My hard sense on culture & money:

To the degree that what I'm saying disgust you, or argues, or makes you ourseon — to that degree the world holds a proven place in our life — has become a God — to that degree we we been dropped by that maleuaterli myth

"Spirit without measure". One of our known faith healers in this country recently died — it was reported grandcoholism. Those appointed to mays who, I'm sure, were helped by him, be must be careful in judging, however, for we don't know his problem. Somewhere there was a flaw in his character as to mind?, your. That's when to show a reasoning out to us, we cannot be trusted with carte blanche? Of divine power

THE WIND OF THE SPIRIT

THE WIND
OF THE
SPIRIT

JAMES S. STEWART

Blow, winds of God, awake and blow
  The mists of earth away:
Shine out, O Light Divine, and show
  How wide and far we stray.
                    J. G. Whittier
"The wind bloweth where it listeth."

ABINGDON PRESS
Nashville and New York

Standard Book Number: 687-45644-4

Library of Congress Catalog Card Number: 69-18447

PRINTED AND BOUND BY THE PARTHENON PRESS, AT
NASHVILLE, TENNESSEE, UNITED STATES OF AMERICA

TO

ALL MY FORMER STUDENTS

OF

NEW COLLEGE, EDINBURGH

with gratitude and affection

ACKNOWLEDGMENTS

Some of these studies have already appeared in print, and for permission to include them here I am grateful to the editors and publishers of *The Expository Times, The Sacramental Table, Sermons I Should Like to Have Preached* (ed. Ian Macpherson) , and *Best Sermons* (ed. Dr. Paul Butler) .

Acknowledgment is due to The Trustees of the Hardy Estate and Macmillan and Co. Ltd. for permission to quote from "The Impercipient," taken from the *Collected Poems of Thomas Hardy;* also to Mrs. George Bambridge and Macmillan and Co. Ltd. for permission to quote from "Mother O'Mine" by Rudyard Kipling, taken from *The Light That Failed.*

CONTENTS

I

THE WIND OF THE SPIRIT

"The wind bloweth where it listeth, and thou hearest the sound thereof, but canst not tell whence it cometh, and whither it goeth: so is every one that is born of the Spirit." —St. John iii. 8.

TO ANYONE BROUGHT up in the Jewish tradition, it was natural, almost inevitable, to compare the Spirit of God with the wind. For in the Hebrew tongue the same term was used for both. The word *ruach* stood in fact for three things. It meant breath, that most impalpable part of existence, the breath of life. It meant also the desert wind, tearing violently across the land with primal energy and elemental force. And it meant the Spirit of God, the supernatural power that sweeps across the ages, and bursts into history, and takes possession of the lives of men.

Now here was Jesus with Nicodemus on the Mount of Olives. It was night, with the moon riding high above Jerusalem, and driven clouds scudding across the face of the moon. The wind blowing up from the valley was stirring the branches and rustling the leaves of the olive trees. Jesus was speaking to Nicodemus about the work of God in the soul and the new birth — how God could take a life that was conscious of failure and emptiness and dissatisfaction and sin, and transform it and make it full and strong and vital and victorious. But Nicodemus was not understanding. He – a master in Israel, a theologian

9

[handwritten: to Charlene as Sharp]

and an accredited leader—found this kind of talk beyond him. So Jesus took an illustration. And Jesus did not need to search far for His illustration that night. It was there, asking to be used. "Listen to the wind, Nicodemus! Listen to the wind! You can hear its sound—the night is full of it, hark to it in the tops of the trees—but where it has come from and where it is going no man knows. Now, Nicodemus, the Spirit of God is just like that— invisible yet unmistakable, impalpable yet full of power, able to do wonderful things for you if only you will stand in its path and turn your face to it and open your life to its influence. Just listen to the wind, Nicodemus! Listen to the wind!"

Now what is Jesus saying here to us? We will break this text up into its component parts, and see.

First, this. "*The wind bloweth.*" That bare, simple statement affirms *the ceaseless action of the Spirit*. This indeed is the basic fact of life. Never has there been a time, never a moment, when the Spirit of God has not been actively at work.

Look at the Bible. It is there on the first page. "The Spirit of God moved upon the face of the waters": the Lord God brooding over the chaos that was to become a world. It is there on the last page. "I am the bright and morning star. And the Spirit and the bride say, Come." So from the beginning of days to the last syllable of recorded time, the wind blows—the Spirit of God is at work. "Whither shall I go from Thy Spirit?" cries a psalmist. "I can ascend to heaven, and He is there. I can make my bed in hell, and He is there. I can take the wings of the morning or hide in midnight—but He is there." God never lets go. If God did let go of this universe for an instant, if God withdrew the action of His Spirit, the whole complicated structure would disintegrate and fly apart like a shattered mirror into a million fragments. It is the Spirit who holds human life together. Never does He cease working. The wind blows.

Of course, the New Testament goes beyond this. The New

Testament says that at one particular point of history there was a sudden new irruption of the Spirit into human life. Jesus, in whom the whole power of the divine Spirit had been focused, had died and risen from the dead in the mightiest of all the Spirit's mighty acts; and now, upon the Church that called Him Lord, there burst the mighty rushing wind of Pentecost. In other words, those men felt the sudden start and shock of being possessed by the identical power that had been in Jesus, and was now and for ever inseparable from Jesus. And still from that moment to this, "the wind bloweth" — sometimes a gentle zephyr, sometimes a judgment hurricane, sometimes a quiet guiding voice in the hour of meditation, sometimes a fierce tornado casting down strongholds of the powers of darkness in the name of Christ — always the Spirit of God at work!

No doubt, there have been times when men have been heard lamenting that God had deserted His creation and left it to its own confused, corrupt devices; times when, in faith's eclipse, Elijah's scathing words about Baal seemed almost applicable to the Lord of heaven — "Cry aloud, for he is a god: either he is musing, or he is on a journey, or perhaps he is asleep and must be awakened." "God sits in heaven and does nothing," grumbled Thomas Carlyle. And H. G. Wells in his last testament, which he called "Mind at the end of its tether," declared man to be played out, the world jaded and devoid of recuperative power, and the only possible philosophy a stoical cynicism. Some of us may have felt like that about our own lives occasionally. "Where is the blessedness I knew when first I saw the Lord? My soul is at the end of its tether — I have nothing to show but the shabby rags and tatters of my mistakes. There is no rebirth nor refreshing anywhere for me." Some are feeling like that about the Church: Where is the hope of revival now? But — listen to the wind, Nicodemus! Listen to the wind, Carlyle and Wells and all you pessimists and cynics! And O my defeated and discomfited soul, listen to the wind, the music of the dawn wind of

Easter and Pentecost! Bless the Lord that through all the chaos of the world, through all the complexities of your own life, God's Spirit is for ever active. On that fact depend all our hope and expectation. In the blackest night, if you open the windows and listen, you will hear the wind, and know that God is stirring, never slumbering, never resting, never desisting from His work of providence and redemption; and His cosmic patience is the salvation of the world.

Second: "the wind bloweth *where it listeth*." If the first affirmation was the ceaseless action of the Spirit, this is *the sovereign freedom of the Spirit*. Just as it is impossible to control the wind or dictate to it its direction, so no man, no Church, can domesticate the Spirit of God or delimit His sphere of operation.

Men have always wanted to do that. They have drawn their rigid dividing-lines and said, "Here is the area in which grace will be valid – in this church, this sect, this racial group, this method of evangelism, this pattern of mission, this old-time religion, this newest of new theologies. Outside this sphere, no salvation!"

This is the perennial temptation of institutional religion. In fact, it is the temptation of all our work for Christ: to imagine that our way of doing things in the Kingdom of Christ is the one and only way, and to be impatient of every other.

But God is for ever upsetting our neat logical schemes and discomfiting our tidy regulations.

Watch how it happened in Jesus' day. Judaism said :"We are the covenant people. We will have no truck with Gentiles and barbarians and lesser breeds without the law. No salvation outside Israel!" And they stood there doggedly, and built high and strong their wall of partition. And then one day, out of the darkness of Mount Calvary, from the red dawn of an empty tomb, there arose a great wind of the Spirit that battered on that wall and levelled it to the dust. With a crash that startled the world the wall of exclusion went down like matchwood before the gale of Pentecost.

There are men working overtime to rebuild it today, with their policies of segregation and their monopolies of grace. Let them beware! The wall will go down again before the tornado of the truth of Christ, and it may bury beneath its ruins those who try to build it.

Always that elusive and intractable Spirit of God keeps embarrassing our preconceptions. For example: why should Rahab the harlot find a place in the great panorama of Hebrews xi and in the ancestry of Jesus Christ? Surely, we protest, that line should have been preserved impeccable! Why should Christianity offer the world an image of God all mixed up with a carpenter's bench and a wayside gallows, this appallingly unphilosophical "scandal of particularity"? Why should providence bypass Athens and Rome and Alexandria, and locate the Saviour of the world in the drab provincialism of Nazareth — "can any good thing come out of Nazareth?" Or pass down the centuries. What a shameful thing, cried the prim sticklers for ecclesiastical etiquette of John Wesley's day, what an utterly disreputable thing, to cheapen religion by carrying it outside the church walls where it belonged, and defiling it in the common concourse of the streets! Rank heresy!

But that is God's way. "The wind bloweth" — not where we timidly suggest or dogmatically demand that it should, not where the most up-to-date computer decrees — "where it listeth." Try shutting the door against it, setting your shoulder to the door and barricading it — and it will break the door down: as on the day when they rolled a great massive stone against the mouth of a tomb in a garden, and sealed it fast, and said, "That's Christ finished! This dead and defeated man will trouble us no more. Let him sleep behind the stone for ever!" Suddenly came the wind of heaven and burst the tomb, and Christ went conquering through the world.

13

Don't try to tame that intractable wind. No act of Convocation or Assembly can circumscribe it, no arrogant political dictator curb it, no rooted personal prejudice patronise it. It is master of the world.

And — don't you see? — this is the essential optimism of Christianity. Here in the Spirit of Christ is a force capable of bursting into the hardest paganism, discomfiting the most rigid dogmatism, electrifying the most suffocating ecclesiasticism.

This is the sovereign freedom of the Holy Spirit. There is no citadel of self and sin that is safe from Him, no unbelieving cynic secure beyond His reach. There is no ironclad bastion of theological self-confidence that is immune, no impregnable agnosticism He cannot disturb into faith, no ancient ecclesiastical animosities He cannot reconcile. And blessed be His name, there is no winter death of the soul that He cannot quicken into a blossoming springtime of life, no dry bones He cannot vitalise into a marching army. This is the glory of Pentecost. "The wind bloweth where it listeth." Come, Holy Spirit, come!

Third: "the wind bloweth where it listeth, *and thou hearest the sound thereof.*" This is *the indisputable evidence of the Spirit.* When the wind is blowing, it makes its presence felt. You hear its sound. You do not need a lecture on the dynamics of atmospherics to tell you that something is going on. That is palpable, unmistakable.

So with the work of the Spirit. When the Spirit of God stirs up a church or an individual or a community, there are palpable evidences of His working. Even the unbeliever becomes aware that something is going on. He sees the effects. He hears its sound.

This indeed is what had brought Nicodemus to Jesus at the first. Nicodemus was not a disciple. He was a Pharisee. He belonged to a group that was naturally antipathetic to Jesus and biased against the gospel. But he was an honest man, who kept his ears open, and he had heard the wonderful things that were happening wherever Jesus went. That is written here into the story. "Rabbi," he exclaims, "no man could do these mighty works you do unless God were with him." In other words, although Nicodemus knew little or nothing about the dynamics of the Messianic revival then stirring Palestine, at least he had heard its sound. He recognised the indisputable evidences. And it was that recognition which, leading him to seek an interview with Jesus, was the first step in his salvation.

Look at it again on the larger scale of the apostolic age. The hard supercilious pagan world of Greece and Rome professed itself indifferent to the gospel; but it could not deny that wherever Christ's men went strange things kept happening. The true life of those Christians was indeed, as Paul declared, a hidden life. "Your life is hid with Christ in God." But it was not all hidden. No! Unconcealed and open were the Christians' impact on society, their revolutionary ethic, their amazing courage amid the vicissitudes of life, their absolute serenity face to face with death. The world, says the Book of Acts, saw the evidences: it "took knowledge of them that they had been with Jesus".

Always there are unmistakable signs when the power of the Spirit goes to work. "Thou hearest the sound thereof." When a man once weak and shifty and unreliable becomes strong and clean and victorious; when a church once stagnant and conventional and introverted throws off its dull tedium and catches fire and becomes alert and missionary-minded; when Christians of different denominations begin to realise there is far more in the risen Christ to unite them than there can be anywhere else in the world or in their own traditions to divide them; when religion, too long taboo in polite conversation, becomes a talking-point again; when decisions for Christ are seen worked out in family and business relationships; when mystic vision bears fruit in social passion – then indeed the world is made to know that something is happening. Something vital is going on. And it is not romanticising to say that we can thank God that all around us in these days the evidences are so indisputably clear. "The wind bloweth where it listeth, and thou hearest the sound thereof." If you have heard that sound, as I hope you have, you can refute all the minimising and depreciating voices in your own heart and in the world around. It is the unanswerable argument for Christ.

Fourth: "thou hearest its sound, *but canst not tell whence it cometh*." This is *the inscrutable origin of the Spirit*.

We all feel a certain element of mystery even in the physical wind. We cannot tell across what immense tracts of land and ocean it has made its way, nor in what atmospheric upheavals it took its birth.

So with all great movements of the Spirit. Where have they sprung from? Can you track down the factors that brought them into being? The Church, the Body of Christ—did that really begin as a committee meeting in Jerusalem, with Peter in the chair, appointing sub-committees to draw up a constitution? The conversion of Saul of Tarsus at the gates of Damascus— can that be represented, as some would have us believe, simply in terms of sunstroke or epilepsy or neurosis or brain-washing psychology? When Peter made his great confession of Messiah-ship, was Jesus just being mythical when He replied—"Flesh and blood have not revealed it to you, but My Father in heaven: it came to you out of eternity"? Where did the Wesleyan movement begin? Was it in the Rectory at Epworth? Or in the Holy Club at Oxford? Or in the meeting-house in Aldersgate Street in London? These are only very partial answers. Better say it began far back in the counsels of eternity. "Thou canst not tell whence."

But some do not like having to make that admission. Some want to eliminate the element of mystery and the dimension of transcendence. They would prefer to have the Father in heaven image replaced by a statement about human self-awareness. Perhaps Nicodemus himself had something of this temperament. He wanted everything explained. He was a theologian who came near losing the living God behind the abstractions of academic debate: not an unknown occurrence even today. "How can a man be born again when he is old?" asked Nicodemus. "Can he enter a second time into his mother's womb? Tell me precisely how this rebirth happens." It was not that Nicodemus was insincere. He just wanted a rational explanation. Where did regeneration come from?

So we rationalise and psychologise and demythologise – until the Christian faith has ceased to be good news about a living personal God acting in history and has become merely something about man and his nature, his so-called authentic existence; until theology has lost itself in anthropology; until perhaps we reach the point of the self-confident journalist who wrote – "We now know there is no such thing as the supernatural." How astonishingly naïve! How frightfully callow! As if there were nothing more in this world than our logic could measure or our intelligence explore! As if man's self-awareness were the soul and centre of the universe! Jesus here says to us, as He said to Nicodemus – Stop explaining, and worship! Stop arguing, and adore. What you have to do is not to tell whence the wind comes – that you will never know. What you have to do is to get your sails up to it, now that it is there: not elaborately to expound its mysterious dynamics, but gladly to yield to its living power. This is the one thing that matters. This is the appeal of Jesus, and this the challenge of Pentecost.

Fifth and finally: "thou canst not tell whence it cometh, *and whither it goeth.*" This is *the incalculable destiny of the Spirit.* You cannot tell where He is liable to carry you.

The gale that blows across the earth in days of storm drives on into the unknown. And no man can tell where the Spirit of God in Christian discipleship may lead him before his life on earth is done.

Here was Nicodemus. Nicodemus did not know that night that the wind of the Spirit was going to carry him one day – do you remember where? To Pontius Pilate's council chamber, to claim the body of Jesus – one of the boldest actions in the gospel story – and beyond that to the world-shattering event of the resurrection. The little group of men in the upper room at Pentecost did not know that the wind of the Spirit that was shaking them was going to carry them and their descendants to the presence of Caesar and the conquest of the world. The monk Martin Luther pondering the epistle to the Romans did not know that the wind of the Spirit stirring in his monastery cell was going to carry him to the revolutionising and remaking of the Church. And today, Christendom with two thousand years behind it does not know where the wind of the Spirit is going to carry it in the next two thousand or twenty thousand years – to what new strength of unity, what triumphs of mission, what redeeming impact on the total life of man. And for the individual – for each of us today – this incalculable destiny of the Spirit stretches out before us.

In some ways it is a daunting, even frightening thought. Perhaps some of us would think twice before praying for the gift of the Spirit if we knew where He was liable to lead us. The Spirit comes on a young man, a medical student who has just taken a brilliant University degree and seems all set to become in the course of the years a consultant at the top of his profession – the Spirit disrupts his plans for a career, and sends him out as a medical missionary to Africa on a miserable pittance. The Spirit comes on a girl immersed in the ordinary, innocent pleasures of life, and she begins to feel constrained to witness for Christ in shop or factory, University or social set. The Spirit comes upon a church, proud of its venerable past, justifying

18

itself by its meritorious history, and compels that church to take seriously the radical word of Jesus – "He who saves his life shall lose it; and he who loses his life for My sake" – and that includes the church that is prepared to lose its life – "shall find it." It is a daunting thought, this incalculable destiny.

But it is thrilling too. For you see, it means you just cannot tell what God may yet make of your life and character. The one thing you must never say is – "My course is fixed and set and circumscribed: no chance of anything fine or noble now for me!" Never – unless you are prepared to "make God a liar" – never under any circumstances say that. It is so atrociously untrue. For Christ at Pentecost and every day is holding out marvellous prospects for everyone – all the drabness and tedium vanquished, all the suffocating poisonous atmosphere of disillusionment gone with the wind of His refreshing grace. And this is not all. For beyond the hopes of earth gleams the incalculable destiny of the hereafter. "Now we are the sons of God, and it doth not yet appear what we shall be. But we know that when He shall appear, we shall be like Him; for we shall see Him as He is."

If only we would take Christ at His word today! If only the Church, if each of us, would allow the Holy Spirit to have His way with us! I know the difficulties. I know all too well the towering, formidable difficulties. But I also know that in the last resort it is as simple as this: will I take Jesus at His word? Now is the accepted time. Listen to the wind, Nicodemus. Listen to the wind!

> And so the shadows fall apart,
>   And so the west winds play;
> And all the windows of my heart
>   I open to Thy day.

2

HOW TO DEAL WITH FRUSTRATION

"It was in the heart of David my father to build an house for the name of the Lord God of Israel. And the Lord said unto David my father, Whereas it was in thine heart to build an house unto my name, thou didst well that it was in thine heart. Nevertheless thou shalt not build the house." — 1 Kings viii. 17-19.

ONE MAJOR FACT in life which we all have to meet is the experience of frustration. How to deal with frustration, how to manage it in a truly Christian way — this is one of life's critical tests.

Consider, first, *the varied forms frustration takes*. Let me mention briefly four.

To begin with, there is the frustration of some specific hope or plan. You decide on a certain course of action — and then the way is blocked. You plan some cherished project, and the plan gets broken. You set out towards the open door of the goal of your dreams, and life cruelly slams that door shut in your face. Here is a man who wanted to make a success of his business, and other bigger firms have come along and crowded him out. Here is someone who longed to travel and see the world, and he is tied all his life to an office-desk. Here is a woman who was engaged to be married, and the war came, and her lover never returned. Many a biography has to record instances of such definite and particular frustrations.

Second, there is a more general form the experience takes. There is the pervading sense of frustration which comes to be diffused across the whole of life. There is the beating of the wings of the eternal spirit within against the bars of irksome limitations, hampering circumstance, all the inevitable handicaps of life, physical, intellectual, social. Here we are, held rigidly in that bondage from which we cannot break clear, with life inexorably hastening past, with a thousand realms of beauty and truth lying round us unexplored in nature, literature, foreign travel, scientific knowledge – all the things we shall never do nor have a chance to do in this world, all the lovely experiences we are missing and can never hope to see. It is a wonderful thing to stand in some huge library like the British Museum, but it can be subtly depressing too: all this vast store of knowledge I shall never acquire! Someone in an office gets ten days' holiday to Switzerland. Marvellous! – but just enough to be a reminder of the thousand lovely scenes, beyond one's reach. Who does not understand the poet's mood?

> To leave unseen so many a glorious sight,
> To leave so many lands unvisited,
> To leave so many worthiest books unread,
> Unrealised so many visions bright; –
> Oh! wretched yet inevitable spite
> Of our brief span, that we must yield our breath,
> And wrap us in the unfeeling coil of death,
> So much remaining of unproved delight.

This is the second form of the experience, this general, pervasive frustration.

The third form is what we encounter in the realm of character. How splendid the brave resolves we often make – how pathetic and disappointing the reality! How the natural, corruptible self within us mocks and thwarts our vows to live

21

for Christ! "The good that I would, I do not; but the evil which I would not, that I do." It is the cry of the frustrated in every age. Why cannot I reproduce the love and trust and self-forgetfulness of Jesus? Why cannot I snub the devil more effectively? All this dull tedious monotony of defeat—who shall deliver me? This is the third form of the experience: frustration in the realm of character.

There is a fourth form—and this we are experiencing acutely today: frustration of our dreams of a new world. "When this war ends," so we told ourselves away back in the years of battle, "we shall take care not to make the mistakes we made last time. We shall set ourselves to build a wonderful new temple of brotherhood and humanity. When the tumult and the shouting die, then—Glory to God in the highest, and on earth peace!" But look at it now—the heaving unrest across the earth from end to end, the chaos of acrimony and estrangement and suspicion.

You remember how in the first glowing enthusiasm begotten of the French Revolution, when youthful spirits everywhere were building wonderful dream temples of liberty, equality, fraternity, Wordsworth cried:

> Bliss was it in that dawn to be alive,
> But to be young was very heaven!

But the years passed, and the vision faded out in sordid disenchantment; and, confessed Wordsworth,

> I lost
> All feeling of conviction, and, in fine,
> Sick, wearied out with contrarieties,
> Yielded up moral questions in despair.

There are many who are hovering on the brink of that reaction today. Is this the wonderful new dawn of concord and goodwill that was to break like an apocalypse upon the human race? Must the dream temple always be sabotaged and wrecked? Why this perpetual frustration?

So much for the main forms the experience takes. Let us pass on, in the second place, to consider *the Bible and frustration*. For this experience is a Bible problem. Again and again within the Word of God you will find men wrestling with this very thing.

Moses stands on Mount Pisgah after forty years of desert wandering, looking across the Jordan at the Promised Land of which through all these weary years he has been thinking, the Canaan of his dreams, the land flowing with milk and honey. "O Lord God," he cries, "let me go over, let me tread the good land beyond Jordan. I have waited for this for forty years – wilt Thou refuse me now? Let me go over!" But God replies, "Enough! Ask Me no more – speak not of this again." And there, within sight of the goal he has struggled towards through half a lifetime, he dies in the desert, shut out, frustrated.

Or again, God calls Jeremiah to be a prophet and a preacher, and the man goes out with the dream of an Israel reborn – only to encounter, as the years go by, the baffling indifference, the unimaginative stolidity and hostility of men. "O Lord, Thou hast deceived me, and I was deceived." The dream is frustrated!

St. Paul plans to launch a great campaign in Bithynia, right on the shores of the Black Sea, dreams of an Asiatic empire for his Christ – I wonder, supposing Paul had gone there, and then on into what is modern Russia, if the world would have been different today – but some inscrutable providence confounds his strategy, bars that door of hope against his entrance, drives him off the other way. Frustrated!

It was the dream of a New Jerusalem, says the writer to

the Hebrews, celebrating the heroes of bygone generations, it was the vision of a city with foundations which inspired those men in every age, and drove them out as pilgrims and sojourners, and urged and lured them on: and "these all died, not having received the promises", not one of them having attained the Zion of their hopes. Yes, the Bible knows all about frustration — this Bible which tells of Jesus Himself weeping over the city that rejected and insulted Him, and crying "O Jerusalem, Jerusalem, how often would I, and ye would not!"

But rarely can there have been a more poignant or dramatic instance than this of our text. Here was David. All his life it had been David's firm and settled intention to give God a home in the very heart of Zion, to erect in Jerusalem a shrine which would be the focus of the national faith and the goal of a thousand pilgrimages:

> To this the joyful nations round,
>   All tribes and tongues, shall flow;
> Up to the hill of God, they'll say,
>   And to His house we'll go.

Even in the heat and fury of his wars, even when disaster had driven him as an outlaw from the throne, this high hope had flamed within his soul. "I will not give sleep to mine eyes, or slumber to mine eyelids, until I find out a place for the Lord, an habitation for the mighty God of Jacob. Arise, O Lord, into Thy rest; Thou, and the ark of Thy strength. For Thy servant's sake turn not away the face of Thine anointed. For the Lord hath chosen Zion: He hath desired it for His habitation. This is My rest for ever: here will I dwell; for I have desired it." Now at last the wars were over, and the land was bathed in the sunshine of prosperity and peace, and the way seemed clear; and with all his characteristic vehemence he set himself to the realising of his ideal, to the translating of it into stone and lime in the magnificent structure which was to be the crowning achievement of his reign and the glory of Mount Zion for ever. And God said — "No! You shall not build the temple. Other hands shall build it, when you are dead and gone." The heartbreaking mystery of frustration!

What are we to say about it, not only as it concerns David, but as it concerns ourselves? Let us rather ask, What does God say? This brings us to our third point: *the divine adjudication of frustration*. The narrative gives the answer. God says this — and, mark this well, for it is a flash of light from heaven across the darkness of many a sore enigma today — God says it is a great thing to have seen the vision, even if your eyes may never in this world behold the fulfilment. "Whereas it was in thine heart to build a house unto My name, thou didst well that it was in thine heart."

Do try to feel the force of this. All through that chequered life of David's, with its splendour and its sin, its glory and its shame, there had been this unquenched longing to serve the Lord his God, this passion to build a House in which the honour of the Lord would dwell, a sanctuary for the strength and beauty of Israel. And this was the thing God fixed upon, saying, "There is a man after Mine own heart!" This — not the man's moral lapses and calamitous, colossal blunders, but this abiding vision — was the saving fact, for it showed the trend and direction of his life. And God spoke the words: "Thou didst well."

Here it may be necessary to guard against a possible misunderstanding. This is not by any means a glorification of good intentions as such. There are people who always intend well — and leave it at that. They will visit that sick friend some day; they will write those letters some day; they will work out their commitment for Christian stewardship some day. They will even dream of getting right with God some day. Meantime they drift. Do you remember St. Augustine? He heard a voice calling, "Awake, thou that sleepest, and arise from the dead, and Christ shall give thee light"; and drowsily he murmured "Anon, presently! Leave me but a little while." He could even pray, "O God, make me pure, but not yet." It would be a tragic distortion of our text's true meaning to suggest that good intentions of this kind are all that God requires. Emphatically it is not saying that.

But having cleared such misunderstanding away, we can return to the positive divine arbitrament: "Thou didst well that it was in thy heart." In other words, to you and me comes the message: Do not let the world destroy your visions or rob you of your dreams. We have not yet been able to build in our generation that long wished for temple of the most high God, an earth of justice and equity and social righteousness and brotherhood, a temple to the honour of the God of peace and love. We have not built it yet: but it will be an awful day for humanity if we lose the driving hope of it, if we allow the frustrations we have experienced once, twice, a score of times, to beat us down into cynicism and despair. It is against this collapse of nerve and faith and hope that the Bible seeks to arm us. "Whereas it was in thine heart to build, thou didst well that it was in thine heart."

Hold to the vision. There will always be cynics who deride idealism. Speak to them of a United Nations Charter to include eventually all nations and all races, speak to them of the Christianising of the life of a secular society, of the eradication of war, of the evangelising of the world—and they will call it sentimental fantasy. "If only these Christians were not such hopelessly unrealistic visionaries! If only they would come down to earth!" It was thus they taunted Christ. Jesus preached a Kingdom which was not a success story, but the bearing of a cross: and they said—"What a fantastic philosophy of life! Did

26

ever anyone hear such unrealistic politics as this? Crucify
Him!"

Fools that they are, and blind in their folly! They have not read
enough history to know that visions can be the most powerful
things on earth; that again and again it has been the man with a
vision – an Archimedes, a Christopher Columbus, a William
Wilberforce, an Abraham Lincoln, a David Livingstone, a
John Mott – who has arrested the drift of centuries and changed
the destiny of the world.

Don't let them rob you! We have not yet built to the glory of
God the great world temple of international righteousness and
peace that is to be, we have not evangelised the earth in this
generation: but it would be a disaster if we lost the hope of it.
That would indeed be the death-blow of civilisation and the
ultimate disloyalty to Christ. "Whereas it was in thine heart,
thou didst well!"

And do remember that just as all this applies to our visions
of a nobler world for the sons of men, so it applies also to our
longings for a more Christlike character for ourselves. We have
not yet come anywhere near building a life on the lines of the
example of Jesus Christ. But if ever a day should come when we
lose the inspiration of that high intention, may God have mercy
on us then.

"I have not attained," cried St. Paul near the end, "it has
been one frustration after another; but, God helping me, I still
press towards the mark!" The man had kept his vision. "We
are all poor sinners," says the writer to the Hebrews in effect,
"thwarted and stumbling in our course again and again, but at
least let us keep running the race with patience, looking unto
Jesus!" This is the essential vision. "I have sinned against
heaven," thought the poor disillusioned lad in the far country,
"I have sinned unpardonably; but perhaps my father will love
me enough to have me back into the home, even if it is only as a
hired servant. I will arise and go!"

27

I cannot chain my soul; it will not rest
In its clay prison, this most narrow sphere;
It has strange impulse, tendency, desire,
Which nowise I account for nor explain,
But cannot stifle.

There is a marvellous text in Micah which John Bunyan has used most dramatically in the description of his pilgrim's terrible fight with Apollyon. Christian, thrown again and again by Apollyon, is struggling doggedly and indomitably to his feet. And he is crying: "Rejoice not against me, O mine enemy; when I fall, I shall arise!"

Don't let life rob you of it. There are moods and taunting voices that will come to you: "You a follower of Jesus! You to aim at Christlikeness, to think of building your life into a temple of the Lord! The thing is absurd." Yes, folly and absurdity perhaps: but be a fool for Christ's sake, and keep that hope in your heart. And though the vision may have been a thousand times frustrated, though it may never on this side of death be realised, hold to it yet. Don't believe them when they tell you that the ethereal vision is a mirage and nothing more. Far better "the half of a broken hope for a pillow at night" than a comfortable semi-cynical philosophy. Far better than the prudent acceptance of defeat is the indomitable cry, "Rejoice not against me, O mine enemy; for when I fall, I shall arise." "Whereas it was in thine heart, thou didst well."

Such is the divine judgment: and this is precisely what the New Testament calls "justification by faith". This phrase – the historic battleground of the Church's witness in bygone ages, but now difficult and abstract to modern ears – stands for the basic truth that God assesses a man's relationship to the Kingdom of Christ, not by the point he has reached on the highway of holiness, but by the way he is facing; not by the distance of his pilgrimage, but by the direction of his life; not by the question, Has he achieved an ethically complete and rounded character,

28

but by the question, Has he his face to Christ, or his back? The ideal of Christlikeness may never have been attained or anything like it, but is the ideal there? Defeated a thousand times, have you kept the vision? This is what God sees, and by this alone God judges. This is the justifying faith that makes the sinner right with God. "Whereas it was in thine heart, thou didst well!"

Notice, finally, *the triumph over frustration*. See how David capitalised the thwarted desire and turned the frustration to glorious gain.

There are some people who, when their dearest hopes are thwarted, grow rebellious. They become embittered, with nerves on edge, railing at providence and mad against the government of the world. Some go even further, and tamper with the divine purpose and seek to force God's hand: "I must and will get my own way," they declare, "even though I have to interfere with the 'divinity that shapes our ends' and cut my pathway right athwart the decree of heaven—I am determined to get it!"

Not so David. If his heart's desire were to elude him for ever, if he were to be gathered to his fathers with the dominant longing of his life unfulfilled, God's will be done. "I refuse to be disappointed," wrote that splendid missionary James Hannington, when bitter opposition was wrecking his dreams for Africa. "I refuse to be disappointed—I will only praise." The man who speaks thus has found the true fulfilment which transcends frustration, the life that is life indeed. For in His will is our peace.

But David did more than acquiesce. He knew now that he would never build the temple: but—and this surely reveals the essential quality of his spirit and the gallantry of his nature—he would spend the rest of his life facilitating the task of those who would come after him.

Who would true valour see
Let him come hither.

A man of lesser breed might have said – "If I am not to do
this thing, that is an end of it – I have no more interest." But
David said – "What can I do now to help the future generation
to which the great achievement will belong?" And we know
what he did. From all over the land he gathered expert crafts-
men. He amassed materials. He arranged contracts for stone
and timber, iron and silver and gold. He laid the foundations.
With all his heart and strength he toiled for this temple which
God had told him he would never see.

This is what Christ's missionaries have done in many a land
and many an age. They have sacrificed themselves and died
without a name, that others might rear upon their forgotten
dust a living temple of the Lord; they have gone forth weeping,
bearing precious seed, that the next generation, or the next again,
might reap the harvest home. Where did they learn it? From
Christ, who did precisely that on Calvary!

Something like this is what we must be doing now, if future
ages are ever to build this war-torn world into a temple of the
Lord.

"Lord," cries the great poet of the ninetieth psalm, "let Thy
work appear unto Thy servants, and Thy glory unto their
children." The work to us – the glory to our children! Give us
the sacrifice, the discipline, if need be the unfinished symphony
and the frustrated hope; give them – our children, those unborn
generations that are to be – give them the happier day, the
nobler heritage, the kindlier world!

To use life thus is to find here and now, through all apparent
frustration, our destiny's true fulfilment. For mark this well.
When the magnificent sanctuary stood complete at last on the
mount of Zion, men called it Solomon's structure; but it was
really David's achievement. Solomon could never have done it,

if David had not prayed and sacrificed and toiled and kept the vision constantly before his eyes and trusted in the Lord. The late Archbishop William Temple in a historic utterance declared that the emergence today of "a Christian fellowship which now extends to almost every nation" is "the great new fact of our era". And he added: "No human agency has planned this. It is the result of the great missionary enterprise of the last hundred and fifty years." In other words, the world Church of the twentieth century could never have arisen if, generations ago, little groups of Christians, fired with the passion of Christ's redeeming love, had not toiled at a task that often seemed desperately unrewarding. "These all died in faith, not having received the promises, but having seen them afar off and were persuaded of them." Under God, what our eyes see today, this great new fact of our era, is their – not our – achievement. Therefore we in our turn, with the fair dream of a world of righteousness and brotherhood and peace to beckon and inspire us, ought the more urgently to make it our prayer: "Let Thy work appear to us, Thy glory to our children". If we cannot build the temple, let us make sure at least that they shall have a foundation to build upon. And "other foundation can no man lay than that is laid, which is Jesus Christ".

There is a most moving letter which is quoted by that distinguished war correspondent Alan Moorehead, at the end of his book on the final stages of the war. It is a letter which a Jugoslav patriot, knowing he was about to die, wrote to his unborn son. Here are the closing sentences: "Now I know I must die, and you must be born to stand upon the rubbish-heap of my errors. Forgive me for this. I am ashamed to leave you an untidy, uncomfortable world. But so it must be. In thought, as a last benediction, I kiss your forehead. Good-night to you – and good-morning, and a clear dawn."

So speaks the patriot to his child unborn. But there is another, even nobler patriotism – the patriotism of the Kingdom of

Jesus Christ. "If I forget thee, O Jerusalem, let my right hand forget her cunning. Walk about Zion, and go round about her; mark ye well her bulwarks, that ye may tell it to the generation following." So, looking down the future generations and dreaming of that fairer and kindlier world that will be the temple of the Lord, we too would say to the generations coming after us: You have to stand on the rubbish-heap of our errors. Forgive us for this. We are ashamed to leave you an untidy, uncomfortable world. But — we believe in God. Christ has kindled in us the dream of a Kingdom that cannot die. For the coming of that Kingdom we pledge our toil and prayers and sacrifice till our day on earth is done. And what matter though we pass hence? If God be for the human race, who can be against it? His Kingdom cannot fail. His temple shall rise in glory. The whole world shall be His dwelling-place at last. Therefore we wish you — in Christ's name — a good morning and a clear dawn!

Is that worth working for, and hoping for, and praying for? Because that was in thine heart, thou didst well!

And for ourselves — is the dream of Christlikeness still within our hearts? Standing, as we all stand today, on the rubbish-heap of our own errors, ashamed of our untidy mess of an attempt to live for Christ — do we cling to it through everything? Do we believe that one day, yonder if not here, the matchless promise of God's Word shall veritably be fulfilled: "We shall be like Him" — like Jesus Christ, just imagine it! — "for we shall see Him as He is"?

Incredible? Yes, from any human standard a thousand times incredible of such raw material as ourselves. And yet, if you will receive it, shiningly and triumphantly true! This is indeed "the good morning and the clear dawn". This is the harvest home, with shouts of joy. And for you here and now the voice of the Lord is saying, "Because this is in your heart, you do well!"

32

3 *Thanksgiving*

GRACE AND GRATITUDE

"Were there not ten cleansed? but where are the nine?" — St. Luke xvii. 17.

THE FIRST THING that strikes you, reading this vivid story, is the dreadful aggregation of trouble on that Jerusalem road. An earlier chapter describes a solitary leper accosting Jesus as He passed. But here is the tragic sight tenfold multiplied, a whole colony of misery, an accumulated horror that might have stunned the heart of Christ Himself.

This is what may well daunt any thinking person looking out at the world today — the mass of trouble there. We have our "Christian Aid" schemes: but, we wonder, can they even begin to cope with the world's accumulated ills? Refugees by the million, starving children, war and famine, crime and delinquency, poverty and ignorance, suffering heaped on suffering, till the imagination staggers and the mind is dazed, and people say — "It does not bear thinking of, it is quite out of hand. No one can possibly deal with it, not Governments, not Churches, perhaps not even God."

Well, it is not for nothing that St. Luke has shown us the divine omnipotence in action, not only with the individual sufferer, but with this tenfold dilemma.

There is always a danger that we should be so stunned with

the mass of misery that we forget the majesty of the Master, so bewildered by the vastness of the human problem that we overlook the hugeness of the divine resource.

This is where the writers of the New Testament correct us. Not that they minimise the colossal sufferings and tragedies of life. On the contrary. With St. John they say frankly, "The whole world lieth in the Evil One"; with St. Paul, "The whole creation groans, travails in pain." That is there, quite realistically. But this also these men have seen, and this they ring out as the basic elemental fact: there is simply no limit to God's power to break through transformingly into any situation, and no end to the revolutionising grace of Christ.

What follows? This at the least: whoever may despair of the world, we Christians never can. Do you remember what Rudyard Kipling said about the power of a mother's love to transcend all known limits?

> If I were hanged on the highest hill,
> I know whose love would follow me still.
> If I were drowned in the deepest sea,
> I know whose tears would come down to me.
> If I were damned of body and soul,
> I know whose prayers would make me whole.

If a mother's love can work such miracles, who can possibly delimit the love of God Almighty? If only we would give Him faith — not the usual diluted mixture as before of half-belief and doubt and apathy, but a strong simple faith that really took Him at His word — He would corroborate it beyond our dreams. "Lord, I believe; help Thou mine unbelief."

Let us come back to the ten lepers on the road. "They lifted up their voices and cried, Jesus, Master, have mercy on us." That at least was a rudimentary faith. The whole leper fraternity had heard by this time of Christ's cure of one of their own number. And now – "It happened to him," these ten were thinking, "then perhaps there is hope for anyone. Why not for us?" And they determined to put it to the test. "Jesus, Master, have mercy!"

Note Jesus' reply: "Go, show yourselves to the priests." Why that? The reason is clear. For the priests, as Leviticus indicates, were also the Medical Officers of Health. Medicine and religion were much more closely integrated then than now. If you had recovered from some infectious ailment involving quarantine and isolation, you would apply to the priest – the local M.O.H. – for the necessary health certificate.

What is strange in the story is that Jesus apparently said this before any cure had happened. That, to say the least of it, was unusual.

But at any rate they had faith enough to obey. Certainly they could have refused. They might have stood looking at Jesus in blank astonishment. "Go to the priests? And pray, what is the use of that with our disease upon us still? Why such a fruitless journey?" But no. There was something in Jesus' tones, something in those magnetic eyes, that compelled obedience.

They started off to the priests. And somewhere along that road, says the evangelist, the wonderful thing happened – the torpor and numbness passing away, the flagging strength renewed: "it came to pass, as they went they were cleansed." As they obeyed Christ's plain command, the longed for healing came.

This is so often the way of it still. The great things the Christian religion talks of – life and healing, the integration of personality, the ending of the sense of meaninglessness and anxiety and boredom, the gift of hope and courage, vitality and joy, everything in fact that the Bible means by "salvation" – these things do not come by sitting down and dreaming of them, or by theorising about their possibility. They do not even come by staying on your knees indefinitely and praying for

35

them. They do come by practical experimentation, by getting your feet on to the road of ethical obedience in simple day to day loyalty. I fancy some of us – even if we cannot see the distant scene – at least know the next step we are meant to take, the plain unspectacular obedience God is asking from us at this moment. That is the way to the miracle. "As they went, they were cleansed."

Let us try to imagine it now, as it might have been, here in St. Luke's narrative. A mile or two down the road, that thrilling indescribable moment when they realised their healing: the sudden surge of gratitude, ten voices praising God for Christ the great Physician – "We are clean! O blessed Healer! We must go back and thank Him. Let us retrace our steps without delay and find Him. For out of the depths we cried, and God heard us; out of the darkness of hell, and He has answered us. Come, let us fling ourselves in worship at His feet." And so back they come, all ten of them, chanting their tenfold psalm – until, yonder is Jesus, and they run to Him, and fall down before Him, crying "Blessed Jesus! Heaven-sent Physician! Thanks be to God!"

But no. That is not the story. That is not what the evangelist has to tell. One came back. The rest – ninety per cent – never heard of again.

What is our reaction? Probably to say – "What a pitiable revelation of human nature! What atrocious ingratitude, rank bad manners and discourtesy! Surely this is quite untypical. It is not how people act." Is that how we feel?

Well, we are wrong. This is not untypical in the least. These nine men were more ready to pray than to praise, more ready with petition than with thanksgiving. "Jesus, have mercy on us." That is there in the story all right: but not "Praise, my soul, the King of heaven!"

Is that so untypical? What about ourselves? We are ready enough to run to God with our petitions, ready when things are

36

going badly to burst in on the mercy-seat clamouring hotly —
"Lord, it is not fair! The world is grossly mismanaged, and can't
You do something about it?" So petition outruns gratitude.
"I'll think more of your prayers," wrote R. L. Stevenson to one
who was somewhat querulous in his religion, "when I see more
of your praises!" For "basically and radically", as Karl Barth
has declared, "all sin is simply ingratitude."

We are ungrateful creatures often. Think, for instance, of
the heaped-up blessings of each returning day. Are we grateful
enough for these? There is an excited psalmist who bursts in
upon us crying "Blessed be God who daily loadeth us with
benefits"—He does not dole them out with stinting hand,
but extravagantly loads us with them—this wonderful earth,
and the miracle of being alive, and food and shelter, and love
and memory and hope, and day and night, and summer and
winter. There is just no end to it, cries the psalmist: "He daily
loadeth us with benefits. Blessed be God!" But we? We tend to
accept it as our due, the bare minimum we have a right to
expect, just common mercies.

We had best take care how we use that word "common".
G. K. Chesterton in one place grows positively wrathful with
Wordsworth. It is where the poet speaks of "the light of common day". Don't you dare call it common, cries Chesterton in
effect, that's blasphemous! "What God hath cleansed, that call
not thou common," said the angel to Peter. We love to sing, in
the twenty-third psalm,

> Goodness and mercy all my life
> Shall surely follow me.

Perhaps we sing it all too easily. Do we realise that if God were
to withdraw His goodness and mercy for one day, one hour,
one moment even, we could not live? "Everything's grace,"
cries one of Stevenson's characters in *The Ebb Tide*, "we walk

37

upon it, we breathe it, we live and die by it, it makes the nails and axles of the universe!" Indeed, we are not nearly grateful enough for the mercies of every ordinary day.

And beyond this, what about the signal deliverances we have known, the miraculous answers to prayer, the dramatic interpositions of a loving providence — are we grateful enough for these? "O God," we prayed in the hour of darkness and the nightmare of anxiety, "if You will help me now and here, now 'while the nearer waters roll, while the tempest still is high,' if You will stand by me and bring me through, I will serve You with my life for ever." And God did help us, brought us through most wonderfully; but that vow we made, where is it today? Forgotten.

Still further, beyond the daily mercies and the dramatic deliverances, what about the stupendous facts of our historic faith — are we grateful enough for these? For God's mighty acts in our redemption? Take the basic statements: "God was made manifest in the flesh. He bore our sins in His own body on the tree. He is risen. He hath abolished death. All things are yours, and ye are Christ's, and Christ is God's." As Christians, we accept that. But — are we astonished by it? Are we thrilled? Has it ever overwhelmed us, blinded our eyes with tears of gratitude?

I wonder if those nine who went their way are so very untypical after all?

Let us follow this a stage further. Suppose we ask: Why did they not return to give thanks? Perhaps they felt that they deserved the miracle; that the health given back to them was no more than their human right. "If there is a God in heaven," they felt, "He should never have allowed us to suffer as we have done all these bitter years. And if He has now thought better and removed it, are we to thank Him for such a tardy act of justice? For restoring what should never have been taken away?"

Perhaps that was their feeling. For human nature, even today, even in us, is always tending to claim that it deserves – "my rights" – things which are God's sheer grace. Have I deserved my health, when the hospitals of the world are full of sufferers? Have I deserved the human love and affection which have cheered me on my way? Have I deserved to be born into a Christian land of freedom? Have I deserved the miracle of divine forgiveness which has been my salvation? If I know anything at all, it is this, that not one of these gifts have I deserved: they are all the unmerited grace of heaven. In fact, that is what the word "grace" means: something completely and for ever undeserved. It is a humbling thought indeed.

That may have been why the lepers failed to return to give thanks: they felt they deserved the miracle. Or perhaps it was not that, but this: other things were more pressing – Christ could wait. There were such urgent matters to be settled. After all, they had been segregated, ostracised, quarantined all these years. Would anyone want them now? Would there be a place waiting for them, when they returned to claim it? Would there be any offer of employment, any work to do? These were the questions they had to get answered: Christ could wait. And in the event, He waited so long that He was quite forgotten. "Where is He now? We don't know. Where was He going? We forgot to ask. What shall we give Him? We had not thought of that." That may have been the way of it. It is often the way of it today. We do not mean to be ungrateful or irreligious, but – well, look at life: it is not our fault, is it, if we are preoccupied, too burdened with multifarious tasks to have much time for things unseen, too inextricably involved in life's hectic rush to think of going to God and giving Him our love? Who was that knocking at the door? Christ? Oh, that's all right. Christ can wait!

So we find reasons why they did not return. We have rationalised our own attitude in the same ways often. But what did

Jesus think about it? Listen to this poignant word that has rung down the centuries. "Were there not ten cleansed, but where are the nine?" That cry still echoes through the crowded ways of our modern world, right into our own streets and homes today. Where are the nine? Were there not ten houses in that street, and one was glad when the Lord's Day came and the bells called to worship – but where are the nine? Were there not ten blessings the love of heaven heaped upon that life, and one has taken root and borne some harvest – but where are the nine? Were there not ten deliverances wrought for that man, and one has stayed in memory – but where are the nine? Were there not ten secret messages that stirred his conscience, and one has not quite gone with the wind – but where are the nine? "O Jerusalem, Jerusalem," cried Jesus once, "how often would I, and ye would not!" That hurts Christ, really wounds Him.

> Blow, blow, thou winter wind,
> Thou art not so unkind
> As man's ingratitude –

to God! In Christina Rossetti's passionate outcry: "Earth, earth, earth, thy cold is keen!" "I am come," declared our Lord, "to send fire upon the earth. But oh, how slow it is to kindle!"

So here in the story the general mood was "Christ can wait." But there was one man who said, "No – Christ shan't wait! The priests, they can wait. My chance of a job, my place in the world, can wait. But not Christ! Not the grace and love that saved me! And if you nine will not come back with me this moment and find Him, and offer yourselves as His disciples, it is rank treason. Christ shan't wait – not the blessed Healer to whom I owe it all!" One came back to tell his gratitude. "I love the Lord, because He hath heard my voice and my supplications. Because He hath inclined His ear unto me, therefore will I call upon Him as long as I live."

His way of telling it was significant. He fell down on his face at Jesus' feet, and "with a loud voice glorified God". Perhaps it was not really necessary to be so demonstrative. He could presumably have done it more unostentatiously. He did not need to startle the echoes with his loud doxologies. We don't like those vulgar hallelujahs. Well, that is our loss, not his. This was a man redeemed; why should he not glorify God with a loud voice — not with the diffident apologetic murmur that is sometimes all we can muster, as though it were not quite seemly to make a joyful noise to the Lord, not quite cultured to be too deeply moved even by the love of Christ? This man had no such illogical inhibitions. There was another day when some good religious folk said to Jesus — "Master, rebuke your disciples. Check those unseemly Hosannas!" Swift as an arrow came the reply: "If these should hold their peace, the stones would immediately cry out!" And if I have no heart to praise Him after all He has done for me, the very stones of the street might well find tongue and shout the praises I have failed to render. "With a loud voice he glorified God."

"And he was a Samaritan." That Luke doubly underlines. A Samaritan — that is to say, an outsider, an alien from the Israel of God. In fact, when he turned in his tracks to go back to Christ, I fancy the other nine all said "Let him go: we are better without him. He is not of our class, not even a Jew, a half-breed, a miserable Samaritan!"

Is it not extraordinary how often the unlikeliest folk are the first to respond to Jesus? Our Lord Himself comments on it here: "They are not found who returned to give glory to God, except this stranger." In Africa, there is a leper colony where two thousand turn out for the weekly prayer meeting. Two thousand! And we are glad if we can get twenty. "Except this stranger." That is the way of it so often. In Jericho there were any number of worthy religious people: why had it to be a Zacchaeus, that more than dubious character, who took Jesus home to dinner? Why had it to be a woman off the streets who anointed Him for His death and burial? Why had it to be twelve rough, uncouth fishermen and others to form the nucleus of a world religion?

> God moves in a mysterious way
> His wonders to perform.

And Christ calls the strangest, unlikeliest folk to be His helpers and disciples. That is important. It means, you see, there is some chance for us.

So let us end our study today, not with the indifference of the nine, but with the gratitude of the one. If that ninefold apathy hurt Jesus terribly, just see how this one man's devotion cheered and gladdened Him. It was a lonesome world for Jesus then, cold, critical, hostile: so that real loyalty, when He did come upon it, was something that touched and moved and strengthened Him—just as the angel, we are told, strengthened Him in Gethsemane.

I put this question to you now, as I put it to my own soul. Do we realise that our poor stumbling words of devotion can cheer the soul of Christ? That our broken tarnished bits of loyalty can make a difference to our Redeemer?

In case we should not believe it, it is written clearly all over the gospels. Why did He choose twelve men at the first? "That they might be with Him," say the evangelists simply: which means that somehow it helped, Him in spite of their blundering obtuseness, in some mysterious way it encouraged Him to have those friends of His around Him. And so through the last terrible week He kept returning every night to the healing peace of the home at Bethany. And so He asked Peter and James and John to stay beside Him in Gethsemane. And so, one feels sure, on the road to Calvary His love ran out towards Simon of Cyrene who eased His burden and carried His cross the last stage of that dreadful journey. And so, dying at last forsaken, there came to Him through the darkness and roar of the swellings of Jordan one tribute of recognition and devotion from a wretched creature hanging there beside Him: "Lord, in Thy kingdom remember me." I verily believe that, hearing that, Christ's heart leapt up, for it meant that He was not going out defeated and forsaken; that here was the beginning of the salvation of the world, and all God had promised from the travail of His soul was coming true already; here was the first instalment of the final victory.

All these – the dying thief and the Cyrenian, the Bethany family, the blundering disciples, and this poor nameless leper with his grateful heart – were God's reinforcing messengers to the Lord Jesus Christ.

I ask again – did you realise that you could do something like that for the Christ who has done everything for you? That your gratitude and loyalty really mean that to God?

And lest anyone should not quite know how to set about it or where to begin, let me remind you that Jesus Himself has made it very plain. "Inasmuch as you do it unto one of the least of these, you do it unto Me."

This is the dynamic motive of "Christian Aid". It is one thing to be temperamentally kind-hearted by nature; but it is quite another thing to aid the suffering because you are seeing Christ stretching out His hands to you in every starving child, every war-victimised sufferer, every friend of your own who is unhappy or forlorn.

Dr. Theodore Ferris has told a story of a traveller out in Africa watching a nun dressing the wounds of a leper. The wounds were revolting, gruesome and repulsive. As he watched her, he said, "I wouldn't do that for ten thousand dollars." She looked up at him, and said, "I wouldn't either." She was not doing it for all the dollars in the world. She was doing it for love, for gratitude to One who had loved her and given Himself for her. "Inasmuch as you do it to one of the least, you do it unto Christ."

It is this unbounded love and gratitude which must be the motivating dynamic of Christian aid and action. In the memorable, moving words of Charles Kingsley in a letter to his wife: "Must we not thank, and thank, and thank for ever, and toil and toil for ever for Him?"

It would be a wonderful thing if from this congregation today, and from every Christian soul, there went up to God a great new surge of gratitude and thanksgiving. "Bless the Lord, O my soul, and forget not all His benefits": who has crowned you with loving-kindness and tender mercy, who goes on daily loading you with gifts beyond all deserving – bless the Lord indeed! And, O my soul, turn your unpayable indebtedness into dedicated service, for the sake of those who need your help, and for the love of Christ your Saviour.

4

THE RELEVANCE OF WORSHIP TO LIFE

"The four and twenty elders and the four living creatures fell down and worshipped God that sat on the throne, saying, Amen; Alleluia." —Revelation xix. 4.

WE HAVE COME in to this sanctuary today to worship God. The world around is full of wars and rumours of wars, and no one knows what may be coming on the earth: but we are here today to worship God. We have come to this place along very different roads of circumstance and experience; I suppose that no two roads that we have travelled through life have been quite identical: but here we are today to worship God. Perhaps the journey has not been easy for some of us recently. Perhaps we have been having to cope with difficulties and problems and forebodings and disappointments and temptations. Perhaps life has been besieging us with its complexity, battering us with its fierce enigmas: the ways of providence have seemed mysterious and dark and difficult to understand. As George Meredith expressed it:

> Ah, what a dusty answer gets the soul
> When hot for certainties in this our life.

But at any rate here we are today to worship God.

And the question is: What ought this worship to mean for us in our actual life situation? Shall we be happier, stronger, more resolute, more serene for having paid our vows to the Lord this day in the midst of His people? But let there be no misunderstanding. I am not suggesting that the main object of worship is the effect it may produce on the worshippers. Its object is God, its sole aim His glory. But we want to see just where and how worship and life impinge together; and this, without any descent into a false subjectivism, we are certainly entitled to ask. When we leave this place, what spirit ought our worship to have kindled within us as we go out to face life and all its crowding, clamorous perplexities again?

To this question Charles Wesley in that great and moving hymn which surely goes to the very heart of Christian worship:

> Let saints on earth in concert sing
> With those whose work is done;
> For all the servants of our King
> In earth and heaven are one —

and St. John in the Book of Revelation have a very dramatic answer. It is not the kind of answer we might have expected, but it is all the more arresting on that account. It is this: if you want to learn anything about worship and its relevance to life, try to overhear the worship of the saints in heaven. The Church militant on earth must capture for itself the essential notes of the worship of the Church triumphant.

"I heard," writes John — and, mark you, he was not idly dreaming on a day of summer ease and spiritual complacency (he would have had nothing to say to us in this grim, tragic age of ours if that had been his background): no, he was writing when the shadow of the devilry of the emperor Domitian was on the world, when withering blasts of militant atheism were

46

scorching the earth and the empire was running red with martyred blood, when no Christian's life was worth a moment's purchase and John himself was a prisoner in the mines and in the concentration camp on the island of Patmos — "I heard," he declares out of that background, "the echo of the worship of the redeemed in heaven: they fell on their faces before the throne of God, and cried 'Amen! Hallelujah!' "

Two words. You know what these words mean. "Amen" — so let it be! God's will be done. "Hallelujah" – praise ye Jehovah, praise the Lord most mighty!

John brought that majestic vision of the heavenly worship back with him — why? In order that the Church on earth, the poor, frail, persecution-battered Church he knew, should learn for its own worship something from the worship of its friends in glory; in order that the Magnificat of heaven should not be quite unknown on earth in days of darkness and confusion.

> Some day or other I shall surely come
>   Where true hearts wait for me;
> Then let me learn the language of that home
>   While here on earth I be:
> Lest my poor lips for want of words be dumb
>   In that high company.

So let us listen to it now. Amen! Hallelujah! Two words — and in these two words four notes are present, the four notes which together make up the harmony of worship and the victory of faith.

The first essential note of worship in its relevance to life is *Acceptance of the Will of God.* This is the first characteristic attitude of the soul that worships in spirit and in truth. They stand before the throne and say, Amen. So be it, Lord!

47

John means that those who have passed over to the other side, whatever they may have suffered here on earth, have no rebellion now within their hearts. Here in the thick of the battle it may be difficult to understand; but away yonder in the perspective of eternity they have seen the plan complete. For them the Master's word is verified: "What I do thou knowest not now, but thou shalt know hereafter." And today they know, and are content. "Just and true are all Thy ways, Thou King of saints!" Amen — so let it be!

So they cry back to us from the sunburst of eternity that all is well. And one day, please God, we shall know it too.

But we have to learn it here. And this is where worship can come in decisively to help us. This is where worship and life are linked inextricably together. It can be so difficult, so terribly difficult sometimes, amid the personal strains and complications and lonelinesses and frustrations and griefs of life, to bow submissively to the will divine.

I know there are some who dislike the very sound of such words as submission and resignation. There is a youthful immature theology that would banish them from its vocabulary. "Resigned? Why should I be resigned? That is weak and feeble and sub-christian. Am I to accept the ills of life, and sit submissively with folded hands, and drug my soul to sleep? God forbid!"

All honour to that gallant rebel mood. But — and this is the point — do not let us forget that if there is a false and feeble pseudo-pietistic way of submitting, there is also an acquiescence that is true and beautiful and brave and Christlike.

"O My Father," prayed Jesus with the red agony of Gethsemane on His brow, "if it be possible let this cup pass. Nevertheless not My will, Father, but Thine! Thy will be done. Amen — so let it be."

But we? No. We are different. We see some grim darkness threatening, or some potential catastrophe descending on our dreams, and we want to cry "Don't permit that, God! Never allow it. I couldn't stand it!"

There was a day at Caesarea Philippi when Jesus took the disciples into His confidence. His hour, He told them, had come. He was about to make the supreme sacrifice on the battlefield of the world. It was His Father's will, and He could do no other. Quietly and gently, yet firmly and inexorably, He told them what must be. All of a sudden Peter, listening, and struck cold to the heart by that frightful prospect of losing his Lord, strode up to Jesus. "Master, this shall not be unto Thee! I refuse to say Amen to it. God's will or not God's will—this shall not be!" And if we had belonged to the disciple group then and in the days that were to follow, I imagine we should have said and done the very same. "Come down from that cross, Jesus! There cannot be any will of God in this. Come down!" And then the world would have remained unsaved for ever. "The cup which My Father hath given Me, shall I not drink it?"

And we must learn to say it too. Even when life brings us to the breaking-point, and hurts us fiercely with its cruel enigmas, we must learn to say it too: Amen, so let it be.

Now in worship we do at least begin to learn it. For it is through worship we come to know that there is just one thing needful at such a time. It is to possess Christ. It is to be sure that there beside you in the dark is One who still as in the days of old gathers the lambs with His arm when they have been hurt, yes, even when in their foolishness they have hurt themselves, and carries them in His bosom. O dear kind Shepherd Christ, the darkness is not dark with Thee, but the night is clear as the day!

Which of the two ways is ours? When proud Cleopatra of Egypt faced the wreck and ruin of her hopes, "It were for me," she cried in bitterness, "to fling my sceptre at the injurious gods, since they have stolen my jewel!" That is one way. But there is another; and if you have ever lost a loved one or said good-bye to hope, will you listen to this of William Barnes the Dorset poet?

Since I do miss your voice and face
   In prayer at eventide,
I'll pray with one sad voice for grace
   To go where you do bide;
Above the tree and bough, my love,
   Where you be gone afore,
An' be awaiten' for me now,
   To come for evermore.

Now we pass on to something different. If the first essential note of worship in its relevance to life is acceptance of the will of God, the second is *Commitment to the Purpose of God*. This also was in the Amen John heard across the battlements of heaven. For in this same chapter he has a vision of the exalted Christ riding forth to the conquest of the world, and all the saints in glory streaming out after Him on that high crusade. They rest not day nor night. They follow the Lamb wherever He goes. For them the divine purpose means action fuller and service grander than they ever knew on earth. Amen, Thy will be done — *and help us to do it*. This is the meaning.

And through our worship we must learn this too. For Christianity is not all submission and resignation, though Marx and Nietzsche thought it was — "a slave morality," said Nietzsche, "the opiate of the people," said Marx and Lenin. Blind fools — had they not read history? Had they not seen the risen Christ in every age inspiring action and energy and courage unsurpassed? No doubt — let us confess it — part of the blame for the misunderstanding must lie at the door of the Church itself. For too often Christians have allowed the faith to appear as a reactionary influence in a revolutionary world: whereas the truth is the exact reverse. It is secularism that is reactionary; Christianity, when authentic, is revolutionary enough, as the Book of Acts reminds us, to "turn the world upside down". And indeed, all through the centuries, in the name of Christ men have marched right up to some of the most formidable, virulent social evils, crying "It is not the will of God that we should tolerate this hateful tyranny one moment longer: it is the will of God that we destroy it!" — and there and then the axe has been laid to the root of the noxious tree, and the hideous abuse has crashed to its destruction.

For the will of God is not simply something to be accepted and borne — it is something to be asserted, something to be done. And Amen is not always a sigh — it is sometimes a shout:

> My God, my Father, make me strong,
> When tasks of life seem hard and long,
> To greet them with this triumph song:
> Thy will be done!

Where this note is lacking, there is no true worship.

There was a day when David, having brought up the ark to Jerusalem, summoned his people to a new campaign, and told them of the wonderful destiny to which the Lord God of their fathers was now calling them; and the magnificent passage in Chronicles ends with a sudden irrepressible shout from the whole congregation — "All the people said Amen, and praised the Lord." I can imagine the sound of that great Amen reverberating round the hills and making the Philistines tremble! If we would only say Amen to our own prayers, which means putting ourselves into these petitions, backing up our supplications with the resolution of dedicated lives — "Thy Kingdom come: *Amen!* Thy world be swept clean of war and oppression and racial discrimination and injustice: *Amen!* Bless our foreign missions: *Amen!*

> Move o'er the waters' face
> Bearing the lamp of grace,
> And in earth's darkest place
> Let there be light:

51

Amen!" — if we would say Amen to our own prayers by thus putting heart and mind and will at Christ's disposal, we should go out and crusade for Christ as we have never done before.

This is urgent. For today there are men and communities and nations saying Amen with all their soul to false God-denying philosophies and ideologies, saying it with a mystic fervour and passion. There are nihilistic creeds that have great multitudes of flaming, dedicated missionaries. Will not we Christians then say Amen to the purpose of our heavenly Father — until every Christian is an instrument in the hand of God, every Church member a missionary for the Kingdom of Christ? There is so much land yet to be possessed. There are so many radical reformations still to be achieved, so much shame of war and cruelty and poverty and ignorance and racial bitterness still to banish from the earth.

"What think ye of Christ?" cries Browning in one place,

> You like this Christianity or not?
> It may be false, but will you wish it true?
> Has it your vote to be so if it can?

What a day this would be for the Church if the Amen of faith and devotion were really a shout of consecrated self-commitment: "It has my vote! I am in this unreservedly. Lord, here am I, send me. Amen!"

We pass to the third essential note of worship in its relevance to life. For through acceptance of the will of God, and commitment to the purpose of God, there comes a wonderful sense of *Joy in the Fellowship of God*. "I heard," says John of the Revelation, "the worship of the Church of heaven, and it was Amen — but it was more: it was Amen, Hallelujah!" For yonder where they dwell in Christ they are eternally happy, and all their sufferings and sorrows of this earth are swallowed up in gladness

and felicity. "In Thy presence is fulness of joy; at Thy right
hand there are pleasures for evermore." And if we have lost this
note – and who can deny that many of us have lost it? – it is
through worship that we must recapture it.

It is a very extraordinary fact that all the way through this
Book of Revelation, which was written at a time when Christianity was fighting for its very life, and Christ had His back to
the wall, and the little flock of Christ was being battered with
hideous atrocious cruelties and colossal sufferings, there breaks
irrepressibly the sound of singing.

But that is just Christianity all over. "What is faith?" cried
Tertullian in the third century, and answered his own question:
"Faith is patience with the lamp lit." That is a lovely word,
worth inscribing on the front page of your private Bible. For
this is where the Christian has the stoic and the cynic and the
fatalist utterly and for ever beaten. Patience is stoic: patience
with the lamp lit is Christian. The stoic may talk grimly about
taking fate by the throat; the cynic may shrug his shoulders and
say he "couldn't care less". But it is a different trumpet-note
you meet on every page of the New Testament. Here are men,
to use their own words, "glorying in tribulation", "enduring
longsuffering with joyfulness". Here is not only "Praise to the
Holiest in the height"; here is also "And in the depth be praise!"

But far too much we have lost it. Burne-Jones was present at
the funeral service for Robert Browning. But he said afterwards
that it was too sombre for his liking. It did not seem to fit the
gallant soul whom they were remembering. "I would have given
something," said Burne-Jones, "for a banner or two; and much
would I have given if a chorister had come out of the triforium
and rent the air with a trumpet." Far too much the Christian
Church has lost that lyrical note. "How shall we sing the Lord's
song in this strange land?" we complain. "What room is there
for Hallelujahs in this disillusioning desert of an age, this fierce,
mad, bitter Babylon of a world?" "By the rivers of Babylon,

there we sat down; yea, we wept, when we remembered Zion."

But I recall a day at St. Andrews when I was acting as chaplain to a student conference — very vividly do I remember, and indeed shall never forget it: it was shortly after the end of the war, and there came to us for one night of the conference that great ecumenical leader of the Church in Holland, Dr. Hendrik Kraemer. He had spent some terrible months as a prisoner in a concentration camp, and his face was lined with suffering. He spoke to these young students that night for half an hour, and the whole burden of his message was this: "We Christians must get the joy of Christ back into our religion. We are denying Christ by losing it!"

And certainly real Christians do seem to capture it, don't they?

> What is this psalm from pitiable places,
>> Glad where the messengers of peace have trod?
> What are these beautiful and holy faces
>> Lit with their loving and aflame with God?

There was a modern martyr of the Church, James Hannington of Oxford and Uganda. He was consecrated Bishop of Eastern Equatorial Africa, and toiled there shiningly for Christ until his work was cut short by violent death. "I felt," he wrote in his diary just before the end, "that they were coming upon me to murder me: but I sang 'Safe in the arms of Jesus,' and laughed at the agony of my situation." That is apostolic and Johannine — safe in the arms of Jesus, and laughing at the agony!

"I heard," says St. John, "the voice of the saints of God; and it was Amen! Hallelujah — praise the Lord!" And I pray that even our worship here today may help to bring the joy of Jesus back to some disconsolate heart.

54

But now — what is the deep root of this joy which can sing its Hallelujahs through the darkness? Here we reach the fourth essential note of worship in its relevance to life, the final characteristic attitude of the soul that worships in spirit and in truth. It is *Assurance of the Victory of God*.

John and Tertullian and Hannington and Kraemer were not deluding themselves with rhetorical fantasies and vague emotions. They were not whistling to keep their courage up in the dark. They were rejoicing — John reiterates it all through his book — because of something which had actually happened in history. There has been an advent, says John. There has been a cross. There has been a resurrection. God in Christ has met the powers of darkness at their worst. He has taken their measure, and has triumphed. Nothing has been left undone. Once and for all, atonement has been achieved and death destroyed, and the doors of the Kingdom of heaven flung open wide. Once and for all, God has devised for this ruined world a way out of chaos and damnation. Therefore — be not dismayed! You are fighting a defeated enemy. This is the fact that cannot be shaken. This is the rock of God beneath your feet.

> Thou hast redeem'd us with Thy blood,
>   And set the pris'ners free;
> Thou mad'st us kings and priests to God,
>   And we shall reign with Thee.

Some fifty years after John wrote his book, there was a frightful martyrdom in the city of Smyrna, during the proconsulship of Statius Quadratus. The aged Polycarp, bishop and saint, was brought to his trial. His judge stood before him and cried — "You are to renounce the faith! You are to curse the name of Christ!" But Polycarp made answer, "Fourscore and six years have I served Him, and He never did me wrong: how then can I revile my King, my Saviour?" So they took him and burned him to

55

death in the amphitheatre. But the young Church in Smyrna hurled its defiance in the very face of his murderers; for when later it came to write down in the annals of the Church what had happened, it was very careful to put in the precise date, and it gave it thus — "Polycarp was martyred, Statius Quadratus being proconsul of Asia, *and Jesus Christ being King for ever!*"

Do let us believe our faith wholeheartedly. God so loved the world. Christ died for our sins. He is risen and alive for ever. He has sounded forth the trumpet that shall never call retreat. The kingdoms of this world are become the Kingdom of our Lord and of His Christ, and He shall reign for ever and ever. He is the way, the truth and the life. Whatever our moods of callow scepticism and agnosticism may say, these things stand impregnable and secure. This is the Lord's doing. This is the victory. Surely, then, we of the Church militant who are struggling here on earth and finding the battle often stern and hard and the road much rougher than we hoped, surely we can lift up our hearts amid the shadows and join our voices today with the Church triumphant, and with our own loved ones across the river who are for ever singing the praises of their Redeemer: "O Jesus, King most wonderful, gathering even now Thy Kingdom to Thyself, Thy will be done! Thy praise be sung!" Surely we can say it: Amen, Amen! Hallelujah, Hallelujah!

And to His dear name be the glory.

5

FOOLS FOR CHRIST'S SAKE

"Peter answered Him and said, Lord, if it be Thou, bid me come
unto Thee on the water. And He said, Come. And when Peter
was come down out of the ship, he walked on the water, to go to
Jesus." — St. Matthew xiv. 28, 29.

"We are fools for Christ's sake." — 1 Corinthians iv. 10.

HERE IS A story from the life of Jesus which the early Church
preserved as being immensely relevant to its own storm-tossed
existence. Was Christ really master of the vast, elemental forces
of secularism and unbelief that flooded the world and threatened
to sweep the Church away? Ought they really to take Jesus at
His word? That was the question. Might it not be incredible
foolishness to rate His claims too highly? Or — should they risk
being fools for Christ's sake? Here was a well remembered
occurrence which, as those early Christians realised, spoke
directly to their own situation.

And surely it speaks no less clearly to us today in our contemporary predicament. I know, of course, that there are
Christians who are uneasy about this kind of narrative, because
it tells of miracle. They find the element of the miraculous
embarrassing. Perhaps in this connection it is worth emphasising
that while there is miracle here undoubtedly, it is nothing like

57

so startling and shattering as the most basic facts on which the faith is built: the miracle, for instance, of the incarnation, God made man, which all Christians accept. I suggest therefore that instead of turning away from this narrative we should look at it again, and mark well what it has to say. It may be that as we follow this vivid account step by step we shall hear God through the Spirit speaking to heart and conscience.

Here was this ship, tossed in the fury of the midnight storm: and for the disciples the worst feature of the situation was — Christ was not there.

They had left Him ashore when they embarked. He had taken the road to the hills. He was away spending the night in solitary prayer. He knew nothing of what was happening. How could He know, thought the disciples, that death was on the sea? He was totally oblivious of their peril. "If only Christ were here!"

And that is the real trouble in the storms of life — to lose your touch with God. Do we not know exactly how those disciples felt? In days of decision, when you have to choose your path for the future and seem flung on your own resources in the critical dilemma, when you cannot make up your mind, and no divine guiding voice comes to you through the struggle — "If only Christ were here!" Or in days of stress, anxiety and emotional distraction, when trouble and depression bow the heart and all the world seems dark, and you do not know how you can possibly face what lies ahead — "If only Christ were here!" Or in days of fierce temptation, when the still small voice of goodness and of the spiritual values seems powerless against the wrecking passions of the soul — "If only Christ were here!" Or in days of great darkness and turmoil and confusion among the nations when the whole world seems to be rebelling against God, days when the prevalent scepticism and unbelief and nihilism are beginning to infect your own life, so that prayer is irksome and the sacraments unreal and the words of God's Book ring hollow — "If only Christ were here!"

He is nearer than we think. That night when He was praying among the hills, Jesus had a vision. He saw the frail little boat tossing on the sea. He sensed the sudden fury of the storm. He knew the urgent peril of His friends. "And," says the evangelist, "in the fourth watch of the night He went unto them, walking on the sea."

There are those here today who have encountered Christ on seas as wild and daunting as Gennesareth. For it is one of the big discoveries of life, how stress and need and desolation may bring the Master suddenly near. When the whole world is in confusion, as it is today, a boiling sea of troubles, the Lord is there within the shadows keeping watch, able to compel even "the elements' rage, the fiend-voices that rave" to subserve the purpose of His sovereign will:

> He plants His footsteps in the sea
> And rides upon the storm.

And when your own life is submerged in perplexities and bewilderments, quite borne down beneath them, then is the time to look up and lift up your head: you are in the presence of God.

> Yea, in the night, my Soul, my daughter,
>   Cry, — clinging Heaven by the hems;
> And lo, Christ walking on the water
>   Not of Gennesareth, but Thames!

But the disciples did not recognise Him. Not at first. "What's that?" they cried, peering through the lashing tempest and the dark, "what is it? It's a spirit, a portent of ill omen! It's the spectre of death, the ghost of the grave. It's a demon of the darkness and the night — God, take it away!" "And," says the evangelist, "they cried aloud in terror."

59

Why did they not know Him? But surely, you say, that is obvious. The night was dark, and the ship was tossing, and their hearts were clutched with fear. How could they know Him? And when it comes to that, how can you expect any storm-tossed soul today to sense a divine presence through the mists of calamity and dejection and despair? A very present help in trouble? A phantom of the mind, more likely – wishful-thinking, nothing more. "Take this apparition away!" And all the time it is Christ.

But there was a deeper reason for the lack of recognition. There was the incredulity of unbelief. They looked again at that figure apparently coming towards them across the waters, and they cried – "No living being can do that! It's positively uncanny. It's demonic! No man alive can walk the sea!" And the unspoken thought was, "Not even Christ!"

And so often when the gospel tells us of a living Lord who can come right into any depths of darkness and confusion with His light, and break into any frightful worry with His peace, and invade any moral despair with an immediate dawn of hope, and trample any ferocious waves of trouble into calm beneath his feet – we are sceptical. "These things don't happen," we say, "and the faith that proclaims them is illusory. No power on earth can come to us over that dark sea. Not even Christ!"

It was then that Jesus, hearing the cry of His disciples' incredulity, spoke to reassure them. "It is I – no spirit nor spectre, but Myself – be not afraid!"

So through the darkness comes a voice that steadies and controls. It is not imagination that invents the presence of God when the sea gets rough. The availability of supernatural grace for individuals and for the nations of the world is not the hallucination of a cheap wishful thinking. It is a magnificent, verifiable reality. You have all the saints of all the ages witnessing unanimously to this: "It is the Lord!" He is here in this bewildered generation, here in this frustrated, frightened world, here in this House of God this moment, here in your own needy heart.

Peter at any rate would make sure. With the dramatic impulsiveness of his nature, he determined to put this to the test. "Lord, if it be Thou, bid me come unto Thee on the water." How characteristic of the man! That startling, reckless idea was thoroughly typical. It was Peter all over.

There was no stampede on the part of the other disciples to get to Christ that night. No, indeed. The storm might shake their wits, but at least they had prudence enough to cling to their last security and keep the boards of the ship's deck beneath their feet. And I reckon that when they heard what Peter was saying, and saw what he was proposing to do, they told him what they thought. "Get back into the boat, you fool! Have you taken leave of your senses? The thing's mad—come back!" And if it had ended in tragedy, as in fact it very nearly did, they would have said "We knew it! Just what we predicted. It was inevitable. It was a crazy act, from start to finish!"

Would you agree with such a judgment? There have been commentators on this passage who have censured Peter for behaving in this ill-advised, idiotic way (as they regard it), and who would have us believe that when Jesus said "Come" it was in order to teach this reckless disciple not to be such a fool again. I wonder.

Look again at this man climbing down out of the boat to go to Jesus: is there no place for that impulsiveness in religion? "He should not have done it." Of course, humanly speaking, he should not. And I suppose Mary should really not have shattered her lovely precious alabaster box at Jesus' feet; and the four men with the paralytic friend should not have torn up the roof of the house to get to Jesus when they found all the doorways blocked; and Matthew should not have left his ledgers and his desk and his comfortable income to go off after the

Prophet of Nazareth; and Father Damien should not have exposed himself to leprosy; and Albert Schweitzer should not have buried himself in Central Africa; and Bonhöffer and Niemöller and Kraemer and Lilje and ten thousand others should not have got embroiled with the authorities and brought upon themselves the horrors of the concentration camp; and young candidates for the mission-field from all the churches should not, with the world as it is today, be thinking of leaving home to tread such a lonely, uncertain path. What preposterous, fantastic things men do for Jesus! And yet – take heed that you despise not one of these: for of such is the Kingdom of God!

Not of the cool, calculating, dispassionate spirit whose only watchword is security. "Show me," exclaimed James Denney, "the man who has never in a moment of high feeling spent what he could not justify on economical grounds, and I will show you a man not fit for the Kingdom of God." Not of the tame, dull, conventional religion which shuns the quixotic extravagance of a burning enthusiasm as it would shun the plague – not of these are Christ's dreams fashioned or any spiritual empires built. But Peter – with the storm in his face, and the cry upon his lips "Lord, bid me come to Thee" – here is the man Christ wants: of such have the Christian centuries been made, of such is the hope of Christianity wrought, and of such is the Kingdom of heaven.

Today the Church awaits a new unleashing of this saving folly. And the only thing that can finally inspire it is an overmastering personal devotion. "Peter walked on the water – *to go to Jesus.*" "We are fools," cried Paul, "*for Christ's sake.*" Men will do for love what they will never attempt in cold blood. Do you think Paul will suffer the loss of all things for an existentialist philosophy? Or Mary break her alabaster box for a theological doctrine of atonement? Or Hugh Latimer burn at the stake for a syllogism in logic? Or Livingstone die in Africa for a theory? Or Peter walk the waves for an abstraction? But men and women will do precisely these things for love, for the love of Christ. And that is why the Word was made flesh, and dwelt among us. God gave us Christ, that our whole being might go down before Him.

> Jesus, my Lord, I Thee adore;
> O make me love Thee more and more.

But there was more here than the blind impulsiveness of love. There was the clear insight of faith. Peter looked at that Figure out across the waters, and there came the daring thought — "If Christ can do that, why not I? Is there any reason why I should not attempt what Christ can do? If He can trample the waves of life beneath His feet, is there not grace for me to do it also?"

This is not irreverence: it is faith of the most vital kind. Of course, with us so often it is different. We look at Christ walking the storms, mastering life's troubles, controlling its passions, trampling on its temptations — and it only depresses us. "It is not for us," we say, "to think of doing that." And we begin to excuse ourselves to our own satisfaction. "He was different, this Jesus. Do not all our creeds proclaim the difference? Very God of very God, begotten not made: but we? Frail children of dust and creatures of a day. Easy for Jesus to scale the heights of His own ideals! Easy for Him to keep calm in the midst of trouble, and pure in the midst of sin, and forgiving unto seventy times seven in the midst of injury, and perfect as His Father in heaven was perfect. But we need not try. We cannot hope to follow Him there. If we launch out into the deep of that fathomless sea, we shall only sink. Fancy people like us, defeated daily by dingy, monotonous temptations, setting out to live like Christ! Could any hope be more foolish and irrational, more surely doomed to disenchantment? We had better be content to stick to a more humdrum and manageable morality. Far better stay in the old boat where we are!" "Forgive us," chants the final chorus in T. S. Eliot's *Murder in the Cathedral,*

> Forgive us, O Lord, we acknowledge ourselves as type of
> the common man,
> Of the men and women who shut the door and sit by the fire;
> Who fear the blessing of God, the loneliness of the night of
> God, the surrender required.

And so we thwart God's purpose to send His supernatural grace coursing through our life and through this broken world which needs that grace so badly; and so we remain in the drab mediocrity of defeat, who might be more than conquerors.

Is this romancing? If you think so, I would have you note Christ's reply to this impulsive man. "Peter said, Lord, bid me come to Thee on the water. And Jesus said" – what? "Man, get back into that boat for your life! I refuse to countenance such folly. Do you hear Me? Back – before you drown!" Did He indeed? No. Jesus said, "Come." I beg you to think of that. He sanctioned the man's impulsiveness. He encouraged it.

"Lord, bid me come," said Father Damien to the Christ of the isle of lepers. And Christ said, "Come." "Bid me come," said Albert Schweitzer to the Christ of the African forest. And Christ said, "Yes, come." "Bid me come," says some young missionary candidate today to the Christ of the ends of the earth. And Christ says, "Yes – Africa is in turmoil, Asia is reeling, the Far East has seen the red flames of war and revolution, the world is in chaos and confusion: but nevertheless – come!" I do not know where Christ may stand for any of us here today, across what gap of sundering waters; I only know that if to any of us Christ says "Come" there is only one thing to do, and that is to get down out of the boat and go to Him.

And this applies, not simply to missionary service or big decisions of that kind, but to the whole trend of your life and mine. It applies very specially to the making of character, and the day-to-day fulfilling of the will of God. "Come and do what I am doing," says Jesus. Here is our standard for life, and we dare not accept a less. "The works that I do shall ye do also." An impossible standard? Yes, manifestly impossible. But the whole point of Christianity is the relevance of the impossible – the divine relevance of the humanly impossible. "Come," commands Christ across the waters, "come and master the waves as I am mastering them. You must not refuse the call, saying 'That standard is not for me; it is futile to imagine that I could ever make anything of that high ideal' – for by God's grace you can. And even if you have been defeated a hundred times, even if life has gone terribly wrong and left you wretched and miserable and ashamed – still, come!"

So Christ challenges us to break away from the dull tedious hidebound mediocrity of a conventional religion. So He summons us daily to fresh paths of high adventure, to walk where He walked, to love and trust as He loved and trusted, to serve and embrace the Father's will as He embraced and served it, to make life lovely with the beauty of holiness, gallant with the gallantry of righteousness, and splendid with the splendour of God. Folly? Perhaps. But never forget it is Jesus Himself who sanctions it. "Lord, bid me come." "Yes, begin now – and come!" "When Peter was come down out of the ship, he walked on the water to go to Jesus."

Moreover, this story gives part at least of the secret. As long as Peter kept his eyes fixed resolutely on Jesus, he succeeded in his attempt. As long as his gaze was rivetted there, his course was straight. It was when momentarily his attention was diverted, and he looked at the black terrifying waste of waters around, that things went wrong. "When he saw the wind boisterous, he was afraid." He began to sink.

What does it involve – to be thus centred on Christ? What

does it mean in practice? It means resetting the spiritual compass every day by acts of prayer and recollection and self-commitment. It means deliberately disciplining myself, yourself, to make time daily (as the Bible puts it) to "stay the mind upon God", to lift it up out of all distractions and fix it consciously on Christ, His greatness, His majesty, His calm and peace and power. Nothing in life can touch the man whose eyes are up to Jesus and who is living in fellowship with Him. It is when we stop praying, when we are so rushed and driven and hectic and preoccupied that the practice of God's presence is crowded out, and we try to do in our own strength what can only be done in His — it is then the swirling waves and tides engulf us, and we begin to sink. We have forfeited our security. We have broken contact with Christ.

It is worth noticing the precise form of expression here: it is most significant. "Beginning to sink." That is the crucial point. The thing had not actually happened. It was only beginning to happen. You could not have told that all was not still well with Peter. Outwardly he seemed to be still mastering the waves. But he knew the difference. He knew something was going wrong. He was beginning to sink.

It is that first stage which is so crucial, whether on Gennesareth or on the sea of life. There is often nothing to show for it when a life is beginning to lose stability and go down beneath the waves. The change may be quite impalpable. And perhaps there is someone here today outwardly still prosperous, still captain of his destiny, still walking bravely in the way of God's commandments, still crowned with honour — but he knows better. He is losing grip. His hold on spiritual ideals is slackening. His standards are deteriorating. He has lost the blessedness he knew when first he saw the Lord. No one would dream of saying he has sunk, for he has not: but — this is the crisis — he is "beginning to sink".

Peter suddenly felt it, and knew it: and all at once above the clamour of the tempest he cried aloud — one of the shortest prayers in the New Testament — "Lord, save me!" No circumlocution in this prayer! It flew swift and straight as an arrow: "Lord, help!"

You need no long elaborate explanations to God when life is beginning to get you down. He knows. He understands. One word can bring His grace decisively into action. "Out of the depths have I cried unto Thee, O Lord!"

"Immediately," says the evangelist, "Jesus stretched forth His hand and caught him" — held him up with that powerful right arm, that mighty, rescuing hand that never yet lost any man who felt its grip. "O thou of little faith, wherefore didst thou doubt?" Did you think I would bid you come to Me on the waters, and not give you strength to do it?

And now the Master is looking straight at you and me. "Why is your faith so small? Did you think I would ask you to face the humanly impossible, and not supply the supernatural resources? Did you imagine I would command you to come and commit your troubled heart to Me, and then let you drown for your obedience? Did you suppose I would give anyone a missionary call, and not be there to help and hearten him on his lonely way? Did you think I would ask anyone to come out of the boat, out of the humdrum security of a conventional morality, and walk with Me the fathomless deep of God's great will — did you think I would ask that, and not reinforce him with invincible grace? You of little faith, why did you doubt?"

Why indeed? What has God done, that we should not trust Him more? "If Christianity sometimes seems hard," wrote Evelyn Underhill, "it is the hardness of a great enterprise in which we get great support." "When thou passest through the waters, I will be with thee; and through the rivers, they shall not overflow thee" — no, not even the floods of Jordan at the end.

So the Master rescued His disciple, and they reached the boat, and the storm died down to calm. "Then" — mark this well, the final word of the narrative—"they that were in the ship worshipped Him." And we who, like those disciples, have seen the works of the Lord and His wonders in the deep, who know that God's hand is on the helm of history and of our own individual experience too, may well get down on our knees beside them at the bottom of the boat, ashamed that we have given Him only a fraction of the love and gratitude we ought to have given. "They that were in the church worshipped Him." "Thou hast delivered my eyes from tears, my feet from falling, my soul from death"—that is true. "I shall not die, but live, and declare the works of the Lord"—this also is true. "Marvellous are Thy works, and that my soul knoweth right well"—it is all true. Therefore—to Him who loves us, and can trample the fiercest waves to level calm beneath His feet, to Him be glory for ever.

6

BEYOND DISILLUSIONMENT
TO FAITH

"The mirage shall become a pool." —Isaiah xxxv. 7 (R.V. margin).

ISRAEL IN CANAAN had come to terms with the desert. The *the desert* desert bordered on Israel's lands, encroached on its fertile fields, marched right up to the roots of Olivet and the very gates of Jerusalem. The desert sent the terrible sirocco blowing from the east, carrying clouds of dust and sand across the sun. The desert was the breeding-ground of fierce nomadic tribes which launched their hungry, harrying battalions across the Jordan. The desert had been the training-ground of Israel itself during the forty terrible years when God was disciplining a rabble out of Egypt into a nation and a church: those wilderness years had left a mark on them for ever. Out of the desert had come an Elijah, an Amos, a Jeremiah. In that same desert John the Baptist was to raise the standard of Messianic revival; there the Essene community of the Dead Sea Scrolls was to promulgate its ascetic ethic; and there Jesus, amid wild beasts and ministering angels, was to meet and rout the devil. It was against the constant background of this blistering, haggard wilderness that the people of God lived out their life. It fascinated their imagination, influenced their culture, haunted their literature, and coloured their theology. The soul of Israel had come to terms with the desert.

This, in a deep spiritual sense, is still part of the human task. For we have to live our lives today — how well we know it in this atomic age — with chaos or the possibility of it just over the horizon. There are no wide comfortable margins any longer between civilisation and the edge of doom. Ever since Hiroshima, the world has felt the breath of that sirocco full in its face. And indeed every man has to meet this issue in his own experience. For every pilgrim road to Jerusalem has its bare desolate tracts. Every gathered congregation could provide scores of personal stories of days of darkness and loneliness when life seemed drained of meaning and strength and purpose, barren days of grief and heartache, broken hope and Paradise Lost — each story ending with the words "That was my desert day." It is immensely significant that all the great masters of the spiritual life — St. Augustine, à Kempis, St. Teresa — warn us repeatedly that we must reckon for the day when helpers fail and comforts flee and God seems to withdraw His face, and the wilderness clamps down upon our souls. The Christian must come to terms with the desert.

Now of all the desert phenomena, the Jew would have told you, the cruellest was the mirage. Far away through the shimmering heat the desert traveller would see a bright oasis, tall green palm trees telling of living water. "Now God be thanked," he would cry, stumbling in the direction of his vision, "God be thanked for this great crowning mercy!" — only to find the vision receding, wavering, vanishing into nothing; and there on the bare rocks at last he would lay himself down to die, mocked by that evanescent phantom, and perhaps even hearing in his soul the echoes of a more terrible mockery: "He that sitteth in the heavens shall laugh; the Lord shall have them in derision."

Israel had had this experience of the mirage dramatically in her own natural history. Amid the desolation of the Egyptian bondage there had been born a magnificent dream, the dream of freedom; and the day arrived when that dream seemed to be

70

coming true, and out they went to taste of that living water,
that intoxicating draught of liberty. What happened? Crushing
disillusionment. "Liberty?" they cried to Moses bitterly, "you
call this liberty? Is this the prize we clutched at? We were better
off as slaves. We have been fooled by our dreams. The hope is
illusion, the pool mirage. Lead us back to Egypt!"

This experience — the exact reverse of Isaiah's prediction here
— is indeed one of the most familiar experiences of life.

Sometimes the disillusionment is startling and crashing and
overwhelming. A Napoleon dreams of world conquest and empire, and ends crying:

> Great men are meteors that consume themselves
> To light the earth. This is my burnt-out hour.

A Goethe contemplates at seventy-five the heaped-up prizes
that the world has showered upon him, and writes, "My existence has been nothing but pain and burden, the perpetual
rolling of a rock that must be raised up again for ever." A
Byron masterfully seizes life and compels it to stand and deliver
the gold and jewels of the happiness he craves, but only to confess ere long:

> My days are in the yellow leaf;
>   The flowers and fruits of love are gone;
> The worm, the canker, and the grief
>   Are mine alone.

And in less dramatic ways the thing is happening continually.
The pool becomes a mirage so often. It has done this somewhere
for every one of us. In fact, it is so familiar that if an Isaiah can
come and reverse it that really will be exciting. You remember
how Captain Scott, finding himself forestalled at the Pole, wrote
in his diary — "Good-bye to our day-dreams!" On less heroic
levels hundreds of thousands have said the same. Good-bye to

our day-dreams: perhaps they were too ethereal for this rough, grudging world. Life so often refuses to play up to the heart's desire, and the brave quest ends in disenchantment: so that a Disraeli, with more than a touch of bitterness, could give it as his philosophy of life — "Youth is a blunder, manhood a struggle, old age a regret."

Is this not precisely how many are feeling today about the quest for world brotherhood and peace? Humanity has seen that lovely vision in the distance, the final oasis beckoning across the deserts of a world at war: not so very long ago it seemed quite near, and men were saying, "We are almost there, just on the edge of it now! This is the dawn of the Golden Age, this is the birth of a brave new world." And then came such shattering disillusionment that thousands today have been left in the grip of iron pessimism and cynicism and despair. "What's the use of striving any more? Your dreams of a new world will always betray you in the end. Vanity of vanities, all is vanity!"

But often the experience is more intimate. Are you quite satisfied about your life's vocation, the work you once thought was going to be so glorious and meaningful and worth while? And happiness? Has the fine flower of happiness not been buffeted by the storms and faded by the heat of the day? "Ah," wrote Thackeray at the end of *Vanity Fair*, "which of us is happy in this world? Which of us has his desire? or, having it, is satisfied? Come, children, let us shut up the box and the puppets, for our play is played out." And what about character? How many of us are satisfied about that? We were going to construct something so strong and splendid and consistent, and what a poor shoddy thing it is after all — bits and pieces, nothing more! That dream of character which was going to lead us to living water — O God, it's just mirage!

Yes, if Isaiah can reverse this, it will be exciting indeed.

And religion? Even religion is not immune. The ultimate disappointment of life is the disappointment about God. "He

trusted in God," jeered the rabble on Calvary, flinging their
taunts up into the face of the dying Christ, "He trusted in God
that he would deliver Him: let Him deliver Him now, if He
delight in Him!" And the sting of it was that, to any onlooker
there, God did nothing and no deliverance came and the tragedy
dragged out to the end. "We trusted." said the two broken-
hearted disciples on the Emmaus road to the unknown Traveller
who had joined them, to whom they had been confessing their
dreams about Jesus, "we trusted that it had been He which
should have redeemed Israel." He was to put our wrong world
right: but that is all over — it can never happen now. Dead on a
gallows, that lovely foolish dream we cherished, crucified, dead
and buried once for all.

> The Man upraised on the Judean crag
>   Captains for us the war with death no more,
> His kingdom hangs as hangs the tattered flag
>   On the tomb of a great knight of yore.

This is the ultimate, quite shattering disappointment, when God
Himself disappoints, and the living water of divine grace becomes mirage.

It can be a terrible hour when that final doubt assaults the
soul. "How could I serve in the wards," cries the hospital nurse
in Tennyson's poem, looking at the physical wreckage round
her, "if the hope of the world were a lie?" But supposing the
hope of the world is indeed a lying mirage, when then? If Jesus
Christ is mistaken, if His standards and interpretation of life
are unfounded and illusory, then all our ideals and struggles
are for nothing.

The man who wrote the seventy-third psalm knew something
of the kind. I have done my best to keep straight and true, he
cried, but what is the use of struggling for the right in a world
that prospers the unscrupulous and sends virtue to the wall?

73

"Verily, I have cleansed my heart in vain: in vain have I washed my hands in innocency." The fountain of life is mirage.

And if Jesus Christ is mistaken! If there is no Father of our spirits after all, no regnant and eternal scale of values but only a dingy ethical relativism, no everlasting differentiating standards to claim implicit sway, no finally redemptive efficacy in the cross and the resurrection — then we have taken the hard way needlessly. We are fools to have sacrificed so much for nothing, to have wasted time in prayer when we ought to have known that the heavens were as brass above our heads; fools not to have been eating, drinking and making merry, and finding self-realisation by casting all Christian inhibitions overboard; fools not to have realised that our sins and repentances, joys and fears do not matter a straw. It is all one in the end. And the moral struggle is not worth the strain and effort. Not worth it!

There cannot be many Christians who get through life without meeting that fierce assault somewhere on the road. Perhaps we are meant to meet it. "My hosanna," declared Dostoievsky, "has passed through great whirlwinds of doubt"; and many a man whose faith is impregnable today would say the same. Supposing I have been pursuing a will-o'-the-wisp in accepting the authority of Jesus? Suppose that all this about "Whosoever will, let him take the water of life freely" is just naïve and empty mockery, and the living water a mirage? Was Thomas Hardy perhaps the true realist that day when, looking towards the fellowship of a church in which he could not share, he wrote:

> That with this bright believing band
>   I have no claim to be,
> That faiths by which my comrades stand
>   Seem fantasies to me,
> And mirage-mist their Shining Land,
>   Is a strange destiny?

74

Fantasies and mirage-mist and imagination and illusion – suppose that is the end of the religious quest? Does the dream go out in nightmare at the last?

It is here that Isaiah breaks in so dramatically. With incredible daring he takes that nightmare view of life and the cynical judgment of the world which says that the pool will always turn out to have been mirage, he takes it and reverses it. "No," shouts Isaiah, "it is a lie! Nail it down, and cast it away. And hear the word of the Lord: the mirage shall become a pool!"

What does he mean? And what right has he to say it?

He means this. He says in effect: "I know that life is full of disappointments, wrecks of golden lovely dreams and broken bits of ethereal hopes. I know all that side of it. But this also I know, from history and my own experience, that God is not mocked! In every situation, even when you are feeling disconsolate and desperate, grace reigns; and God's offer to your thirsty soul is not illusory – it really is living water." Mark you, this is not the facile philosophy of a comfortable piety: it is the discovery of a man who had seen life and suffered dreadfully – like Father Damien or Dietrich Bonhöffer – and now wants all the world to share his discovery. "Look!" he cries, "I see it running at your feet today – the living water. O taste and see how gracious the Lord is! Stoop down, and drink, and live." And Isaiah is joined by a great multitude who have tested it and proved it. The fact is, it is the man who thinks he can find happiness in this world without God who is bound for the mirage, heading straight for disillusionment: the one thing certain about the dream of bliss that seeks to circumvent and bypass the law of God is that the dream will not come true. "Thou has made us for Thyself, and our heart is restless until it rest in Thee." Do not fear, then, says Isaiah, to trust yourself to that wisdom and that love, even if the world thinks you are a poor

75

visionary and a fool: you are the true realist, and your hope will not deceive you in the end.

In that lovely poignant tale of African life *Cry, the Beloved Country*, Kumalo the village priest who has suffered much is speaking to Father Vincent. "It seems that God has turned from me," he says. To which Father Vincent replies: "That may seem to happen. But it does not happen. Never, never does it happen." If only we could trust like that!

See how it was proved in Israel's own experience. They were carried away into exile, and they said, "This is the end. The glory is departed. Our hopes are finished. There is nothing left but heartache, misery, death. The pool is mirage." But there in Babylon the miracle happened. There, broken, prostrated and defeated, those homesick exiles discovered God — as not even in the shining days of David and Solomon and the Temple had they ever found Him before. "Yea, though I walk through the valley of the shadow of death and the shambles of Babylon, I will fear no evil, for Thou art there. Yea, though I make my bed in hell, behold, Thou art there!" So a new spiritual faith was born. "Israel went into exile a nation, and came back a church." The mirage had become a pool.

All down the years this has been proved anew. The faith never glosses over the fact that Christ's call means sacrifice and discipline. If there is someone here today hesitating on the edge of Christian faith, someone who has never quite answered the call but is thinking about doing it — it is necessary to say frankly that it will mean strenuous sacrifice and daily discipline. But this is the guarantee: you will make a wonderful discovery, the same discovery which Isaiah and Paul and Bonhöffer and a host of others have made. You will discover the sacrifice to be creative, and the experience of "grace to help in time of need" no mirage, but a magnificent, triumphant reality.

Do you remember a sudden shout that breaks out of the pages of St. John's Gospel, the cry of the eternal Christ athwart the centuries? "In the last day, the great day of the feast, Jesus stood and cried, saying, If any man thirst, let him come unto Me, and drink." And there is that wonderful vision in the Book of Revelation about the Promised Land and the fount of living waters. No doubt the writer was thinking of the world beyond. But I tell you now—there are some of us here today who know we do not need to wait for death to have that great vision come true, for it is happening here and now: "The Lamb, which is in the midst of the throne, shall lead them unto living fountains of waters." He is doing it for us every day!

Oh, I know we lose touch so often, and our vows are brittle and get broken; the yoke and the burden seem depressing. Is Christ forgetting that we are just common clay? The way of discipleship then seems lustreless and without exhilaration; we are a poor, tawdry advertisement of what the Christian faith should be.

But I know, too, how the miracle that came to Israel in exile, and to Isaiah in his disillusioned mood, happens again. I know there are men and women in this congregation who could tell of it convincingly. I know the sudden release and gladness that come when one rediscovers that one would rather be on the most difficult road with Jesus than anywhere else in the world without Him. And I know that if this yoke and this burden are bondage, then—blessed be such bonds, and God forbid that I should ever try to evade them. Lord Jesus Christ, Your yoke is easy, and Your burden is light!

This is the peace of God, the secret of all true zest and happiness and blessing, and it is proof against doubt and disenchantment and the devil. This is the nightmare of disillusionment shattered by the dawn of faith. This is the mirage become a pool.

And we can trust it even though the world deride. St. Teresa in her day had a lovely answer to those who told her that her visions were delusion and mirage. She admitted she might

77

perhaps mistake one person for another. "But," she went on, "if this person left behind him jewels as pledges of his love, and I found myself rich having before been poor, I could not believe, even if I wished, that I had been mistaken. And these jewels I could show them; for all who knew me saw clearly that my soul was changed; the difference was great and palpable." Teresa's hope in Christ was no imagination and mirage; it was a pool of living waters.

Was this not supremely the experience of our Lord Himself? Jesus set out from Nazareth with the dream of winning the whole world for God. And life took that splendid dream and seemed to shatter it to fragments, brutally, ferociously. The world would not have His gospel, the inquisitive, thronging crowds soon dwindled into nothing, His best friends forsook Him and fled, His enemies struck, and He died in the dark alone. The pool had become a mirage. But — and this is the victory — He died believing, quite sure that the shattered dream was still the very truth of God, that God would not leave His soul in hell nor suffer His hope to see corruption: and because of that the cross — the terrible cross — has become the glorious channel of redeeming love. It has veritably been the river of life for millions. "O Son of Man," cried George Matheson, "whenever I doubt of life, I think on Thee!"

> I came to Jesus, and I drank
>   Of that life-giving stream;
> My thirst was quenched, my soul revived,
>   And now I live in Him.

The mirage has become a pool.

Will you not trust this for your own life, with all your particular problems and frustrations and bewilderments and disappointments? There was a day when Francis Thompson, who more than most men had been fiercely buffeted by life and

scourged by its apparent indifference to his dreams, hurt
callously and almost unbearably in the region of his emotions,
who had felt with Job the temptation to curse God and die and
make an end, for everything he valued most seemed lost and
every beckoning vision was mirage, heard a clear voice calling
to him from heaven:

> All which I took from thee I did but take,
>   Not for thy harms,
> But just that thou might'st seek it in My arms.
>   All which thy child's mistake
> Fancies as lost, I have stored for thee at home:
>   Rise, clasp My hand, and come.

And will you not trust it too – that Christ's interpretation of life
was based on no delusion, that He made no mistake when He
set His name on you in baptism and called you to His service,
that His offer to you today of happiness and peace and a satis-
fying life is really valid and substantial, and that the vision He
has set before your eyes will never lead astray?

In our best moments, we all know that. If only we could trust
it always! I remember once near Interlaken waiting for days
to see the Jungfrau which was hidden in mists. They told me it
was there, and I should have been a fool to doubt their word,
for those who told me lived there and they knew. Then one day
the mists were gone and the whole great mountain stood revealed. Next day the mists were back, but now I had seen, and
knew myself that it was true. Men and women, let us trust the
saints, the people who have a right to speak about the fellowship of Christ because they have lived in that country all their
lives. Yes, and let us trust our own moments of vision: what
matter though there are days when the mists come down and
the face of God is hidden? We have seen, and we know for ever
that this is real, so real that by it we can live and die. And if

you are in church one day and they are singing John Newton's words, as we are about to sing them now —

> How sweet the Name of Jesus sounds   ᵘᴸ
>   In a believer's ear!
> It soothes his sorrows, heals his wounds,
>   And drives away his fear —

then even if you have brought a clamouring crowd of doubts and worries and perplexities with you into the church, do tell yourself: This is the abiding reality of life! I have seen it with the mists off, and I know. It was valid once, and it is valid now and for ever. This is what matters most of all. This will stand when all the flowers of every primrose path that lures me from it have withered to corruption.

Will you be saying that as we sing the great words now? The Christian Church has sung them for well-nigh two hundred years, and will be singing them long after we are all gone. And to all who thus rest on the Name of Jesus He comes Himself, travelling in the greatness of His strength, mighty to save. He is here, according to His promise, now — your sorrows to soothe, your wounds to heal, your fears to drive away. Thanks be to God for His unspeakable gift!

Believe on basis of faith / others.

7

CHRIST AND THE CITY

"When He was come near, He beheld the city, and wept over it."
—St. Luke xix. 41.

THERE ARE DIFFERENT ways of seeing the city, any great city—Jerusalem, London, Paris, New York.

The youth in a remote provincial village dreams of the city far away, and sees it as the gateway to adventure. Here, it seems to say to him, is glamour; here are freedom, pleasure, comradeship, romance. The city is often an irresistible magnet when the heart is young.

The ambitious man of business sees the city differently. He sees it as a place for carving out a successful career. What matter if there are smoke and fog and grime and slum properties in city streets? There are fortunes waiting to be made.

Another man uprooted from the country and doomed to toil all his days in the town sees it differently again. He sees the city mainly as a place to escape from. He sees it with the eyes of a prisoner and an exile. Among its towering formidable buildings, its noisy streets, its thronging pavements, its dreadful anonymity, he feels stifled and suffocated, hating his bondage and yearning to be free.

London streets are gold – ah, give me leaves a-glinting
'Midst grey dykes and hedges in the autumn sun!
London water's wine, poured out for all unstinting –
God! for the little brooks that tumble as they run. /

All these are seeing the city from different angles. But now, what is it they are seeing? Not surely the city as it truly is. Not the beating heart of Birmingham or Glasgow or Chicago or Berlin. Not certainly what Jesus was seeing that Palm Sunday when He came over the brow of Olivet and beheld Jerusalem and stood still and wept.

There are different ways of seeing the city. The statistician sees the city as a social unit, comprising so many parliamentary voters, so many Town Council wards, so many new housing sites, factories, industrial estates, art galleries, churches, schools. The poet sees the city as a fascinating silhouette against the sky. He stands in the dawn on Westminster Bridge and cries:

> Earth has not anything to show more fair:
> Dull would he be of soul who could pass by
> A sight so touching in its majesty.

The moralist sees the city as a microcosm of humanity. In *Sartor Resartus* the philosopher sits in his high attic at midnight above the roar of crowded streets. Strange, he reflects, that all around me are those teeming thousands, men being born, men dying, laughing, cursing, hoping, fearing – "but I sit above it all; I am alone with the stars".

There are those different ways of "beholding the city". When Wordsworth saw the city, he grew lyrical over it. When Carlyle saw the city, he philosophised over it. When Jesus saw the city, He wept over it.

This is the difference. And it forces on us the question whether we have ever really stood with Jesus there on Olivet. Have we ever looked as He looked on the crowded ways of men? Have we seen the city with the eyes of Christ?

Of course, there are those who deliberately choose not to see the city as it is. They realise that, if they did, the vision would disturb their tranquillity and might even break their heart. That is why thousands of people can dwell in a city all their lives and never really know it—its gallantry and brotherhood, its solitude and shame.

Here was Jerusalem. I imagine that Jesus was the only one who wept over Jerusalem that day. There were thousands of pilgrims in that Passover season, tens of thousands streaming up to the capital along all the roads of Judaea. What did they see as they came near and looked upon the city standing majestical on the hill, with its towers and battlements white and shining in the morning sun?

Some saw merely the end of an arduous pilgrimage. They were tired, footsore, exhausted. They had travelled a long way. Some, like Simon of Cyrene, had come from Africa; some from Mesopotamia, Macedonia, Rome. Their one thought when they saw the city was—"Thank God we are here at last. Thank God we can lay down our staff and unloose the dusty sandals from our feet. Thank God for the end of the road!"

Others, with more buoyant spirit, saw the city differently. They saw it through the eyes of patriotism and pride. This was the great moment they had been dreaming of for years. There in front of them was the metropolis of Israel. Land of hope and glory! There were the very heights for which David had fought. There were the walls before which the legions of Sennacherib had been rolled back and vanished in the night. If only, they thought, history would repeat itself! If only the same fate might overtake the legions of the imperial tyrant of the west who now held Jerusalem in thrall! Down with Rome and up with Jewry! Defiance to all dictatorships. Shatter the chains and slavery. Jerusalem our mother shall be free!

Others, with deeper penetration and more religious insight, saw the city differently again. They saw it as the focus of a spiritual faith. They saw it as a sanctuary and a shrine. "Dear City of God," they cried, "dear altar of our holy faith! Glorious things are spoken of thee. This is none other than the house of God, and this is the gate of heaven!"

So all those thousands of pilgrims drew near Jerusalem that day, and gazed on it with the most varied emotions in their hearts. Only one pilgrim stood there and looked and wept.

Before we ask what He was seeing that made Him weep, let us pause to remark how moving are those tears of Jesus. It will help us to appreciate this if we consider certain facts.

Consider, for one thing, that they were *the tears of the bravest Man who ever lived*. He was no weakling, apt like some of us to flinch from disquieting facts. He had the heart of a lion and nerves of steel. He was no kill-joy. His most characteristic word was "Be of good cheer," and His voice has always had more music in it for troubled hearts than all the symphonies of the world. He was no sentimentalist. One day when a too emotional follower had cried out as He passed – "Blessed be the mother who bore you and the breast where your head lay," He had turned round at once and rebuked the sentimental speech: "Don't say that! Say rather, Blessed are they who hear the word of God and do it." For the great thing is not to sentimentalise the word of God, but to catch step to its triumphant march.

He was the bravest of all the sons of men; yet here over Jerusalem He weeps. There is always something terrible in the sight of a brave man's tears. David was a brave man: and we feel like intruders in the presence of that paroxysm of weeping, "O my son Absalom, my son, my son Absalom! Would God I had died for thee, O Absalom, my son, my son!" Peter was a brave man: and we bow our heads before that shattering moment of which the evangelists tell, when after his denial he rushed sobbing into the dark—"Peter went out, and wept bitterly." Paul was a brave man: and nothing in Paul's history is more moving than the hour when his friends at Caesarea tried to dissuade him from his last dangerous journey, realising that after this parting they might never meet on earth again; until Paul, unable to bear their pleading a moment longer, broke out with a great sob and cried—"Enough! What mean ye to weep and to break my heart like this?" How tenfold moving, then, the tears of Jesus over Jerusalem, since He was "the Lion of the tribe of Judah" and His far and away the bravest spirit this earth has ever seen!

Consider a second fact: how moving are those tears *when you contrast them with what had gone immediately before*. Then the cry had been "Ride on, ride on in majesty!" For Palm Sunday was a day of pageant, cavalcade and festival, full of tumult and shouting and acclamation. Loud hosannas were still echoing on the morning air. "Hail, Son of David," was the cry. "Christ the royal Master leads against the foe!" The clans were gathering. The tribes were mustering. The King was coming into His own. "Rejoice greatly, daughter of Zion! Shout, daughter of Jerusalem." And Jesus had accepted the demonstration and encouraged it. It was His open challenge and defiance of the powers of darkness. He would ride into His capital as the King of Israel and the Master of the world.

> Follow a light that leaps and spins,
>   Follow the fire unfurled!
> For riseth up against realm and rod,
> A thing forgotten, a thing downtrod,
> The last lost giant, even God,
>   Is risen against the world.

That was the setting. And then suddenly, without warning, this bewildering, incongruous breakdown (as the demonstrators regarded it), this astonishing sight – the royal Son of David weeping, the Warrior-King in tears. How moving is this moment when you contrast it with what went before!

Consider a third fact: how moving are those tears when you reflect that *they mean there are tears in the heart of God*. "He that hath seen Me hath seen the Father." Men in every age have tried to probe the inscrutable mystery of the power behind the universe. Some have thought of it as an aloof intelligence. Some, like Thomas Hardy, have called it a blind indifferent omnipotence. Some, like H. G. Wells, have spoken of a harsh implacable hostility. Some, like the psalmist, have heard across the darkness the echoes of a mocking mirth: "He that sitteth in the heavens shall laugh; the Lord shall have them in derision." But we to whom Jesus of Nazareth is the great revealer and the very character of the eternal have learned the deeper truth. We have stood with Him on Olivet, and we know now and for ever that there are tears in the heart of God, and that the inmost centre of the government of the universe is an infinite compassion. Very vividly do I remember a day in my last charge in Edinburgh when that great American scholar-theologian Reinhold Niebuhr came and preached to us on Romans vii: "I see another law in my members, warring against the law of my mind, and bringing me into captivity. O wretched man that I am! Who shall deliver me?" He showed the logical and rational impossibility of man's extrication from the chaos of his own devising. But Niebuhr finished his sermon that day by declaring that the final fact in the universe is something that might appear downright illogical and irrational. It is the vast, incomprehensible pity of the eternal. "Like as a father pitieth his children, so pitieth the Lord." How moving are those tears of Jesus that have taught us this!

Now comes the crucial question. When Jesus looked on Jerusalem that day, what brought the tears starting to His eyes? Why was He thus visibly distressed? Certainly it was not the thought of His own impending doom. It was no loss of nerve induced by an anticipation of the lash and the thorns and the nails. "Weep not for Me," He was to say to the daughters of Jerusalem; and assuredly He was not weeping for Himself. What then did He see, gazing at Jerusalem, that made Him weep? His own words, recorded here by St. Luke, give the answer. He saw three things.

He saw, first, *the fleeting impermanence of earthly glory*. "The days are coming when thine enemies shall compass thee round, and lay thee level with the ground, and not leave one stone upon another." With His prophetic insight Jesus saw what actually happened there in Jerusalem forty years later, when the red ruin of Rome rained down on the pride of Israel, the temple was razed to the ground, and the city went up in flames. He saw that all Jerusalem's glory lay in the past; that all its great men were gone, "glimmering through the dream of things that were"; that all its pomp of yesterday was one with Nineveh and Tyre. Amid the Palm Sunday shouts and hosannas Jesus heard a deeper undertone, the funeral knell of the city that had thought it was immortal. He saw the rains descending and the floods coming and the winds blowing and beating upon that house built on the sand of national pride; and it fell, and great was the fall of it. He wept for the impermanence of earthly glory.

On what are we basing our confidence for the future of mankind? Every civilisation, every secular society, every national culture, has its day and ceases to be.

> The cloud-capped towers, the gorgeous palaces,
> The solemn temples, the great globe itself,
> Yea, all which it inherit, shall dissolve,
> And, like this insubstantial pageant faded,
> Leave not a rack behind.

The Bible always warns us that "this world passes away".
However alien to our present-day mood the message may be,
however superior we may feel in our emancipation from other-
worldly perspectives, the Bible persists in reminding us – This
is not your home. This Jerusalem is no abiding city. This is
only your bivouac on the march. But the Bible does this, not in
order to plunge us in melancholy and fatalism; not to make us
say with Arthur Koestler, "As long as chaos dominates the
world, God is an anachronism"; but to win us to a surer confidence and a livelier hope; to make us know that, deep as is the
chaos today, "underneath are the everlasting arms".

> Who trusts in God's unchanging love
> Builds on the rock that nought can move.

And what of our own life? Jesus was looking across forty
years in the story of Jerusalem, and seeing the end. How many
years in our life story does He see still to come? Far less than
forty for many of us here. "In the morning, it flourisheth and
groweth up: in the evening, it is cut down and withereth." The
natural man within us builds so feverishly our futile, frail
defences – health, possessions, business stability, financial
security – to keep the inevitable at bay. We try to hold and
perpetuate the fleeting present against the unknown menace
of the future and the ravaging attrition of the years. And Christ,
looking at us, can only stand and weep. "O Jerusalem, Jerusalem, the days are coming when all your natural defences will
break, and destruction devastate your mortal dreams and
write 'vanity of vanities' across the ashes of your secular hopes."
But Christ tells us something more today. One absolute security
remains – even in this world where "all flesh is grass, and all
the glory of man as the flower of grass" – one unassailable fact
abides: "the grass withereth, the flower fadeth, but the word of
the Lord endureth for ever". What, then, have we to do? What

but take that abiding word into our heart, and join our mortal nature to the immortality of God? Nothing can destroy the life in which Christ has His dwelling and His throne.

But Jesus, looking at Jerusalem, saw more then the fleeting impermanence of earthly glory. He saw also *the groping blindness of human ideals.* "If thou hadst known, even thou, at least in this thy day, the things which belong unto thy peace! But now they are hid from thine eyes." Jerusalem was blind to her own interests. She had her values all wrong, her ideals hopelessly confused. She did not know on what her true peace depended. Centuries before, there had been a Hebrew poet who had cried – "Pray for the peace of Jerusalem! Pray for the tranquillity of Zion." And on that Palm Sunday when Jesus stood on Olivet thousands were in fact praying for Jerusalem's peace – but all the time looking for it in the wrong place. The Zealots in their secular conventicles were praying for the peace of Jerusalem; but to them peace could come only through blood and fire and revolution and extermination. The members of the Sanhedrin in their council chamber were praying for the peace of Jerusalem; but to them peace was an affair of political opportunism based on compromise and cunning manipulation of the balance of power. The priests in the temple were praying for the peace of Jerusalem; but to them peace meant placating the wrath of God with sacrifices and ceremonies and church ordinances, conciliating the favour of heaven with mountains of burnt-offerings and altars splashed with blood. The scribes in the synagogues were praying for the peace of Jerusalem; but to them peace could be achieved only through dictated obedience to the traditions of the law. And all of them in their heart of hearts were beginning to suspect that none of their panaceas would give Jerusalem the peace of heaven. The Zealots, even while they fanned the fierce flames of fanaticism and preached a patriotism off the leash of morality, knew that so far from

creating peace they were only precipitating chaos. The Sanhedrin, with all their craft, knew they could not hold the balance
indefinitely. The priests knew that the blood of bulls and goats
would never take away sin. The scribes knew you cannot
pacify a guilty conscience with good works nor make men moral
with a decalogue. In their inmost hearts, they all knew that
Jerusalem's peace was not there; but none of them could tell
where its real peace lay.

Still after nineteen centuries Jesus stands and weeps over the
groping blindness of human ideals. "If you had known, at
least in this your day" — surely after two fierce world cataclysms
in one generation you should have known; at least in this day
when your science has unleashed a force atrocious enough to
engulf humanity and wreck the world — "if you had known the
things which belong to your peace! But now they are hid from
your eyes." Of course, we need for a peaceful world all the
international machinery that has been created; but why is
world peace not coming? We need for a peaceful, prosperous
nation all the social planning of which we are capable: but why
are there such frightful anomalies and injustices still? We need
for a strong united Church all that World Councils and
General Assemblies can devise: but why are we still waiting
for the fire from heaven? We need for a peaceful conscience and
a victorious life all the moral effort we can put into the fight:
but why this dull shoddy mediocrity and monotony of defeat?
Is this perhaps the root of our trouble — that we set out to plan
for peace, security, prosperity, vaguely hoping that somehow,
when we have done it, the Kingdom of God will then be added
unto us? If only we can keep the balance of power between East
and West, the balance of terror in this dangerous world, then
perhaps we shall see the crisis through and God will lead us to a
better day. And on the individual level we say — If I can plan
my life correctly, and deal with all its clamorous demands,
perhaps God will have a blessing for me at the end. Jesus says —

"Your planning is all wrong. Your priorities are fatally confused. You must begin at the other end. Seek ye first the Kingdom of God, and then all these other things will be added unto you." Put God's will first, and peace will follow. And thank God that, even though the eleventh hour has struck, it is not too late.

> Turn back, O man, forswear thy foolish ways!
> Would man but wake from out his haunted sleep,
> Earth might be fair and all men glad and wise.

God, who in Christ has reconciled all things to Himself, can make us the ambassadors of this world-rectifying, life-renewing reconciliation. This is the peace of Jerusalem.

Jesus, looking at Jerusalem that day, saw the impermanence of earthly glory and the blindness of human ideals. This finally He saw: *the urgent crisis of divine opportunity.* "Thou knewest not the time of thy visitation." Do you grasp what our Lord meant by that haunting word, "the time of visitation"? In Jewish theology, it would have meant an encounter with God — probably at death or away at the end of the world. Jesus meant that, in His own person, the confrontation was already taking place. God was now visiting His people. He meant that there and then, in that very moment, the Lord of hosts had come to the frontiers of Israel and the door of Jerusalem, and stood there knocking. This was the urgent crisis, this the divine opportunity: Immanuel — God with us. "Lift up your heads, O ye gates; lift them up, ye everlasting doors; and the King of glory shall come in." And the frightening thing was — they knew not the time of their visitation. They could not recognise God their Saviour when they saw Him. They did not know that God's last redeeming word was being spoken, and that there had come to their very gates that day the Desire of all nations and the Hope of the ends of the earth. This was the tragedy.

But surely it will not be repeated here today. Surely we can stay those tears of Jesus now. For the urgent crisis of divine opportunity is upon us once again. This is indeed our day of visitation. Jesus has wept long over the world, for its blindness and rebellion. He has wept long over His Church, for its complacency, disunity, and remoteness from the life of men. He has wept long over your life and mine, for our un-Christlikeness, our compromising mediocrity, "our weak self-love and guilty pride" that have been His Pilate and His Judas, our cowardice in witness, our pettiness, our dull subservience to the world, the flesh and the devil. But perhaps even Jesus can

> Trace the rainbow through the rain,
> And feel the promise is not vain
> That morn shall tearless be.

At any rate, the marvellous thing is that He has not cast us off. He has not cast our nation off, nor our Church. He has not cast any of us off. Today God is coming to us again, the God of infinite compassion and measureless grace. Here in this holy place, to you, to me, He comes. There is not one of us who has given God a fraction of the love we might have given. There is not one of us who has served Him as we ought. There is not one whose response to the sacrifice of Christ does not need to be reaffirmed, not one who would not be mightily helped by a new definite act of commitment today. If in our conscience He is speaking now — "O Jerusalem, Jerusalem, how often would I, and ye would not! My Son, My daughter, give Me your heart!" — must we not register a fresh vow and a more binding covenant, and then go out to love and serve Him with our life? Then indeed for Christ our Lord, who has cried over Jerusalem, the ancient promise will be fulfilled: 'Weeping may endure for a night, but joy cometh in the morning. He that goeth forth and weepeth, bearing precious seed, shall come again with shouts of joy, bringing his harvest home!"

Am I mistaken in hearing something of that harvest shout of the joy of Christ across the Jerusalem of our baffled and bewildered generation? And across the new Israel which is the holy Church throughout all the world? Yes, and across the citadel of your life and mine, as the Lord God claims His own? "O Jerusalem, Jerusalem, My joy and crown, My temple and My throne!" This is the peace of Jerusalem.

"Even so, come, Lord Jesus!"

8

THE DARKNESS WHERE GOD WAS

"The people stood afar off, and Moses drew near unto the thick darkness where God was." — Exodus xx. 21.

THIS IS THE paradox of life.

"God is light," cries St. John, "and in Him is no darkness at all." "He has rescued us," exclaims St. Paul, "out of darkness into His marvellous light." "Light of the world," sings Horatius Bonar, "undimming and unsetting! O shine each mist away." When God touches a nation, a church, an individual soul, this is the cry — "Arise, shine, for thy light is come! Risen upon thee is the sun of righteousness with healing in His wings."

Yet here stands this: "the thick darkness where God was." This is the paradox.

It says significantly that "the people stood afar off," and left this one man to travel that road alone. They were glad to stand afar off. The further the better! Mount Sinai was grim enough even in the sunshine. But today, with that weird black thundercloud overshadowing it, they dare not go near it. Not in that darkness! Not in that thick ominous blackness. Who knew what demons, what fiends and phantom furies, might have their dwelling there? Stand back! Not one step further! So the whole convoy halted, and left one iron-nerved individual to go on alone. And he drew near into that thick darkness that looked like the abode of doom — the thick darkness *where God was*.

This is the paradox, then and now. And because it thrusts itself inexorably into the very structure of our human life and history, demanding that we should come to terms with it, I ask you to consider it now. The thick darkness – and God!

Take it first on the widest possible scale. Take it on the scale of the world. Take it of *the darkness of history*: that welter of chaos and confusion in which – so at any rate our modern sceptics are for ever telling us, in books and plays, in devastating logic and bitter satire – no living God, certainly no Father Almighty can possibly be. Talk about a loving providence? they demand. What about the millions of miserable homeless refugees? What about the ruthless slave-camps out of sight? What about the huge colossal shadow of the hydrogen bomb poised menacingly not only over this generation but over the hopes and happiness of generations yet unborn? This is the darkness of history: and I say frankly that in face of it any glib and facile religion is intolerable. Any cheap talk about all being right with the world is woefully, shamefully shallow.

But let us go deeper. Let us answer history by history. Take the descendants of those same people here at Sinai – the nation of Israel. There was a day when a terrible thick darkness loomed suddenly upon them, when all the glory of the exodus, all the majesty of David, all the dreams of prophets, seemed utterly eclipsed – the day of exile and disintegration. "By the rivers of Babylon, there we sat down; yea, we wept when we remembered Zion." And when the taunt of the Babylonian tormentors rang out, "Where is now your God?" the real sting of it to the Israelite heart was the horrible suspicion that the taunt was true: that Jehovah had in fact left them to their fate, that wherever He might be – now that His proud temple on the Mount of Zion was a wrecked and gaping ruin – He certainly was not there in Babylon.

But look! Just then the miracle happened. While all the

people stood afar off, helpless and hopeless and miserable, one man (his name was Jeremiah) drew near into the thick darkness, penetrating with magnificent daring into the very heart of this frightful mystery. What happened? This happened: there in that thick darkness he discovered the outlines of a plan and a purpose, a national destiny far more splendid and divine than Israel in her most glorious days had ever dared to dream. The experience of heartbreak and humiliation, this terrible blow to the proud self-consciousness of Israel, this he saw was to become positive and creative, the greatest spiritual force to mould her history. It was the thick darkness of Babylon still, but—so different now—"the darkness where God was".

Or you could think of another hour in history some centuries later. By this time, Caesar in Rome bestrode the narrow world like a colossus; and where was Israel now? A vassal province, a national nonentity, less than the dust beneath Caesar's chariot wheels. And Israel's politicians were appeasers, and Israel's priests were secularists, and Israel's prophets casuists, and Israel's leaders men ready for any massacre of the innocents. And there came a Babe to Bethlehem, a working-man to Nazareth. "He came unto His own and His own received Him not": only the servile cry "We have no king but Caesar," only the unanimous vote for Barabbas against Jesus, only the sordid squalor of the execution squad on the hill of Golgotha, with the sun hiding its face for very shame and darkness at noon over all the land.

But see! Once again the miracle: the miracle of God veritably present where it seemed no God could possibly be, God present there redeemingly as nowhere else in all the world. For the accursed gallows became the altar of salvation, the act of man's consummate devilry the vehicle of omnipotent love. "The thick darkness—where God was!"

And so we turn back to our own contemporary scene. The thick darkness of history! The dilemma of collective evil! The

96

predicament of man! "You ought to know better," the sceptic says to us, "than chatter about providence in a world like this. Where is now your God? Perhaps sitting aloft in some fictitious heaven? Far better be done with that outmoded belief, and try the technique of a militant materialism instead." But that sceptic is wrong. We Christians ought to be confronting contemporary history with seriousness, yes, but without an atom of defeatism.

It is an awful thing to hear Christians, as I have heard them, bemoaning the world as pessimistically as any unbeliever. It is a mortifying thing to meet Christians so obsessed with disillusioning problems that they forget the victory of their Master. Do let us believe our own faith that the God who came to Israel through the thick darkness of the exile, the God who was reconciling the world to Himself in the thick darkness of Calvary, is not deserting the world stumbling through these shadows now. The basic fact of history is not the iron curtain, but the rent veil, not the devil's strategy, but the divine sovereignty. *Sursum corda* – lift up your hearts! The thick darkness – where God was.

But now I move on to something more personal. Turn from history to what is more intimate and individual. I mean that *dark night of the soul* through which almost everyone at some time passes. And here I am thinking not only of the great devastating trials that occasionally strike like a tornado. That is part of it, of course: it may be a failure of business, a loss of health, a shattered romance, the onset of pain, the break-up of a home, the desolation of bereavement. "The people stood afar off," says the text, when this one man went into the darkness – and it is like that still. The people stand afar off: for even with all the Christian love and sympathy imaginable around you at such times, you may feel that you are treading the darkness alone.

But quite apart from these specific troubles, I am thinking

also and even more of that dark night of the soul which is the eclipse of faith, the withering of enthusiasm, the wretched feeling of meaninglessness and emptiness and futility pervading everything: "vanity of vanities, all is vanity."

I am not talking at random: I am talking about what goes on in your soul and in mine. Have you never found yourself, for example, questioning the very basis of your creed? Have you never days when the attempt to pray seems forced and fruitless? We sing the psalmist's words:

> Each day I rise I will Thee bless,
> And praise Thy name time without end.

Is it always true — "time without end"? "I will Thee bless — each day I rise"? Are there not days when life gets you down, the wear and tear take their toll, the hallelujahs of the saints are irritating, the ordinances of religion irksome, the means of grace "weary, stale, flat and unprofitable"? At such a time, "I don't believe," you feel like crying, "I don't believe this jumbled sorry scheme of things makes sense. I don't and can't believe!"

Far be it from me to reproach that restiveness. But I beg and beseech of you not to lose heart in that darkness. For remember — all the saints without exception have had that experience, from Jacob and Elijah right down to Evelyn Underhill and Dietrich Bonhöffer. The brightest and best of the sons of the morning have been there before you. And they all with one unanimous voice bear witness: "the thick darkness where God was." The saints are not liars. This thing is true. Jacob at midnight down in the black savage gorge of the Kedron wrestled with a horrible oppressive shadow, and when the dawn broke he suddenly knew he had been wrestling with God; and that night, that terrible night, became the most incomparably important in his life. He did not only get through the darkness:

it turned the raw ordinary creature he was into what the Bible henceforth calls him – a prince with God.

Don't lose heart in the dark hour! For the God who Himself went through the darkest hour of all to redeem the world is quite certainly there. And every congregation has people in it now who would never have been there today if they had not proved this true beyond the shadow of a doubt: "the thick darkness – and God!"

I pass, in the third place, to something different. What is this text saying to us about *the darkness of sin*? The Bible, you will remember, speaks about people preferring the darkness to the light, actually preferring it, "because their deeds are evil": because in the dark they hope to hide from God. "I will make my bed in Sheol," cries the man in the psalm, "I will say, Surely the darkness shall cover me!" "Judas went out," relates the evangelist, describing the upper room and the Last Supper and the lighted table, "Judas went out – and it was night": welcome night, to cover up his stealthy dark design. It is typical of the Bible's knowledge of human nature that almost its first page gives a picture of a man and a woman hiding from God: hiding in the deep shadows of a garden from a voice that seemed uncomfortably near. "No one need ever know" – this is the argument – "in the secret depths of personality we are alone: not all the glaring lights in the world can pierce that innermost citadel where thought and motive lie concealed!"

Vain hope and utter fallacy! "The thick darkness where God was." "If I make my bed in Sheol," cries the discomfited creature in the psalm, "behold, Thou art there! The darkness hideth not from Thee." Shakespeare was saying the same thing, when he interrupted Macbeth's midnight meditations with the sudden, ominous knocking at the door. Francis Thompson said it in *The Hound of Heaven*:

I fled Him down the nights and down the days,
I fled Him down the arches of the years —

but always hearing "those strong feet that followed, followed after." There is nothing I can think or say or do in the darkness but the pure eye of heaven sees it all. "The thick darkness where God was."

But this is where judgment turns to mercy. This is where the Hound of Heaven becomes the love that will not let me go. "If I make my bed in hell, Thou art there": that is salvation. I think of Simon Peter hiding his tormented conscience on the dark night of his betrayal: it was precisely because God was in that darkness that he came through not an outcast but an apostle. I think of Saul of Tarsus, self-confessed blasphemer, persecutor, murderer, falling suddenly from his horse outside the Damascus gate: it was because God was in that fall that he emerged not a soul in hell but a saint of heaven. And when we have gone our self-chosen way into the darkness we have not shaken Jesus Christ off. It is awful that He should know us as we are, but it is also the source of all our hope and blessing and renewal. If I am a denier like Peter, a self-justifying sinner like Paul, Thou art there — my ever-loving Lord! "The thick darkness where God was."

I have spoken of the darkness of history, the dark night of the soul, the darkness of sin — each of them transfigured by the presence of God. Finally, there is the last dark valley of all: *the darkness of death*. As one grows older, and as friends and companions of the pilgrimage drop out, it is borne in upon one how foolish and how wrong it is to practise the familiar modern subterfuge of pretending death is not there. No doubt some of our forefathers thought about it too much; but crowds of our contemporaries seem determined never to think about it at all. "It is so depressing," they would tell us. "Why should we let that sombre shadow of the future cloud the bright sunshine of the here and now?"

> Ah, fill the Cup:—what boots it to repeat
> How Time is slipping underneath our Feet:
>   Unborn Tomorrow and dead Yesterday,
> Why fret about them if Today be sweet?

But what is wrong with that spirit is this: it has never Christianised its thought of death. Not that the New Testament ever takes death lightly. It would not insult the mourning heart by doing that. The New Testament says death is "the last enemy"; it says it is full of pathos, and finality, and darkness, yes, and solitude. "The people stood afar off," when he drew near into the thick darkness; for when that river comes, we enter it one by one, alone. All this is true. But the Christianising of death by the New Testament is this: "the thick darkness where God is!" And that means, mark you, not slurring over death by some vague generalities about a possible survival, but the shattering of death by the glory of Christ's resurrection. "Now is Christ risen from the dead"—to make the valley of the shadow the gate of heaven. They proved it true—our dear ones yonder in the Father's house today: "the thick darkness where God was." "And all the trumpets sounded for them on the other side."

There was a little child, the daughter of a widowed father, whose last words regularly every night when he looked in to see her were—"Goodnight, father, I'll see you again in the morning." One day she was struck down by illness, and grew weaker, and the trouble was pronounced incurable. Just before the end she looked up again, and the whisper came—"Goodnight, father, I'll see you in the morning." "And with the morn those angel faces smile." Perhaps our Lord's last words on Calvary were not so very different. "Father, into Thy hands I commend my spirit." Perhaps these were words which as a little child He had learned as His nightly prayer, years before in the home in Nazareth at His mother's knee. Now at the very last they were on His lips again: "Father, into Thy hands I commend my spirit." And that presence made the darkness light.

And now when our turn comes He has promised to be there. There is nothing, absolutely nothing, to fear. The darkest road with Christ is better than the brightest road without Him. And — as Clement of Alexandria said very beautifully — "Christ turns all our sunsets into dawns."

9

THE STRENGTHENING ANGEL

"There appeared an angel unto Him from heaven, strengthening Him." —St. Luke xxii. 43.

ON THIS STRANGE journey of life that we are all travelling from the cradle to the grave, the crucial question concerns resources for the road. Are we properly equipped for such an incalculable pilgrimage? Can we be sure we shall hold out to the end?

The question takes many forms. Shall we have faith enough for the big emergency if one day it crashes in upon us? Shall we have hope enough to defy the corroding influence of multiplying years and the cynicism of disillusionment? Shall we have love enough to triumph over all resentments and exasperation, and to keep the fire of a true devotion to God and man burning on the altar when the rough winds of life are threatening to blow it out? On our journey through the world, this question of adequate resources is overwhelmingly important. Have we got strength for the strain?

Days come to all of us when a desolating sense of human weakness and inadequacy sweeps over us. How shall I do if life thrusts me into a crisis I have never met before? How shall I do if one day the mystery of suffering ceases to be an abstract philosophical problem for a pleasant Sunday evening's discussion, and becomes a sudden tornado battering my sheltered comfortable house of life and leaving it a wrecked and ruined heap? How shall I do in the fearful pit of depression and the miry clay of defeat? How shall I do if the road becomes suddenly steeper, rougher, lonelier than I ever imagined it could be, and heart and flesh cry out — "I can't go on! I'm beaten. I'll never manage this"? And at the last, when the gloaming deepens into darkness, how shall I do in the swellings of Jordan?

It is perhaps not surprising that ordinary creatures like ourselves should have such moods. For not even the saints have been immune.

There was a day, for example, when it happened to that rugged, virile man of God, Elijah. The subtle, stubborn scheming of Ahab and Jezebel and the powers of darkness had been getting on his nerves and finally induced a sudden spiritual reaction and collapse. "I'm through with faith and hope and love," he cried in effect, flinging himself down like a peevish, petulant child beneath his juniper bush. "No one cares! Life is not worth living — I wish I were dead!"

There was a day when it came even to the greatest and most sensitive of all the prophets, Jeremiah. Read his twentieth chapter, and see Jeremiah marching up to the throne of grace to resign his commission as a prophet, to put it back into the hands of the God who had given it, feeling that all his endeavour had been abortive and futile and ridiculous. "Don't talk to me of a faithful Creator," he said that day, "don't fool me with shining, specious promises that have nothing in them but words. O Lord, Thou hast deceived me, and I was deceived!"

There was a day when it happened to the apostle Paul. That nagging, aching thorn in the flesh was spoiling everything, dogging him with dull, chronic pain and misery, and cramping all his plans of service. "Why can't it leave me alone? It's getting worse — there are days when it is sheer torment. I can't go on like this indefinitely. O God, for pity's sake, take it away!"

There was a day it came to the disciple Peter. "I've denied my Lord," he thought wretchedly. "This dreadul thing, this unforgivable thing, has happened. Once, twice, thrice I did it. O God, I'm sick of myself! I'm no use now for anything. I'm finished!"

in well doing

> Weary the cry of the wind is, weary the sea,
> Weary the heart and the mind and the body of me!

I repeat, it is not altogether surprising that dull plodding creatures like ourselves should have occasional moods of feeling helpless in the face of life, appallingly conscious of personal deficiency, when even the saints of God have not been immune. It is always bound to be a precarious pilgrimage, this journey through the world. Are our resources adequate?

Faced by that question, we become aware of certain voices from opposite directions offering diverse counsel.

Thus in the modern world there is a whole group of confident voices whose insistent theme is this: "When the testing hour arrives, all you have to do is to bring into action your own latent reserves of power. You possess undeveloped, untapped energies – physical and psychic energies – of which you have scarcely dreamed. Well then, summon them forth! There is no need to be tyrannised by a haunting sense of deficient resources. That can only breed mental ill-health and nervous breakdown. Take a firm grip on your staggering soul! Believe in your own inner light. Develop your own natural resources! This is the way to stand fast in the evil day, and having done all, to stand!"

So speak the confident voices; and no doubt the counsel is valid enough up to a point. No doubt there are these latent psychic energies in every one of us. But do be clear about this: that advice leaves out the whole of Christianity. If that had been substantially the message of the faith, it could never have been called "news", good news. For that is as old as the ancient stoics: Zeno and Cleanthes had said it long before Christ was born. And there are plenty of exponents of a behaviourist psychology saying it today. Christianity says something quite different. It says you can do something far better than look to your own natural resources and trust your own inner light. Natural resources? Man, it says, you can be supernaturalised! And it is no inner light you are left to walk by, but an outer light – fair as the moon, clear as the sun, glorious as an army with banners!

Now this is what the Bible means by its doctrine of angels. The word "angel", *angelos*, literally means messenger, envoy; a messenger from God; help from the beyond; a visitation from the supernatural world, that other world which is no fantasy of the imagination but actually more real than the material world our five senses apprehend; that world which is never far away, but always pressing in upon us, impinging on us; that world we should apprehend and see if our sixth sense, our faculty of spiritual vision, had not become so atrophied through disuse.

So to Elijah, whimpering under the juniper bush, a beaten, broken man, there appeared an angel strengthening him: that is to say, not some inner process of auto-suggestion, some device of the man's own nature, but a real visitation, an influx of energy from the world of super-nature which is the being of God. So to Paul, at the end of his tether with his thorn in the flesh, there came a touch, a voice, an injection of new life from that other world: "My grace is sufficient for thee; My strength is made perfect in weakness." So to the young Covenanting martyr in the Grassmarket at Edinburgh there came on the high terrible scaffold the sudden reinforcing power of heaven. "The angels!" he shouted to the crowd beneath, "Look! The angels! They have come to carry me to Jesus' bosom."

Now it was something like this, declares the evangelist, that happened in the life of Christ Himself.

At the beginning of the story, Jesus went out into the desert to do battle with the devil; and He was there in the solitude with the wild beasts and the angels. What a parable of the fight of faith that goes on incessantly in every generation — wild beasts, and angels, and the soul of man between! "The devil leaveth Him," the evangelists record, "and behold, angels came and ministered unto Him."

Again at the end of the story, when Peter for a moment had recourse to physical violence and drew that foolish, pathetic sword of his to defend his Master from arrest, "Sheathe that sword!" cried Jesus. "Don't you realise I could appeal to My Father, and He would send Me at once more than twelve legions of angels to defend Me — all the might of heaven at My beck and call?" And so we read that here in the garden, when the colossal terrible burden of the sin of mankind was laid upon His loving heart, till the fierce agony of that crushing load made His sweat like blood, there came to the eternal Son the reinforcing power of the eternal Father. "There appeared an angel unto Him from heaven, strengthening Him." And Jesus left the garden that night to face the final sacrifice with a conquering, ineffable serenity, knowing that underneath Him were the everlasting arms.

And to ourselves also, in the time of need, there can come in the mercy of heaven the same wonderful experience. There are those in every congregation who would vouch for it, for it has happened to them.

So let us ask what form the angels take today. How do they come?

Well, for one thing, *the strengthening angel is often some shining word out of the Book of God*. There are some here who could tell how at the crucial moment of strain or fierce temptation or doubt or imminent collapse there leapt upon them — as a message from another world, a sudden shaft of light across the darkness —

a reinforcing, rallying word of God. Do you remember the day when you were down in the depths because life had been so difficult, and you felt you could not keep going much longer but would just have to give in – and suddenly there came to you Paul's trumpet cry, "I can do all things through Christ who strengtheneth me"? Or that other time when a devastating sense of unworthiness swept over you, and you felt utterly ashamed to be called a Christian, being so atrociously unlike Christ – and then against the night like stars there appeared the word: "I have blotted out as a thick cloud thy transgressions, and as a cloud thy sins"? What is that experience but this: "There appeared an angel to him from heaven, strengthening him"?

For this Bible that we commonly ignore is really help from the beyond. It is no dull man-made compendium of religious theories and ideas. It is not one more tedious diagnosis of our dilemma and predicament. It is the real eternal world imping-ing on this world of sense and time. It is supernature breaking into nature. It is a new dimension. It is revelation. It is the strengthening angel.

This was the experience of Augustine, the clever, conceited, sensual young don of the University of Carthage, with his brilliant outward success and his constant inner defeat. To Augustine in the garden at Milan there came a voice – "Take up and read"; and on the first page he opened he read the words, "Put ye on the Lord Jesus Christ, and make not pro-vision for the flesh." Instantly his chains fell off and he was free. "There appeared an angel to him strengthening him" – and that verse from Romans was the angel!

It was the experience of the sixteenth-century Bishop, John Fisher of Rochester. When they led him out from the Tower of London to his martyrdom, he suddenly caught sight of the high scaffold on which he was to die; and for a moment he quailed, and his nerve seemed breaking. But he took his Vulgate Testa-ment out of his pocket, and praying, "O God, send me some special word to help me in this awful hour," he opened it and read from the seventeenth of St. John, "This is life eternal, to know Thee the only true God and Jesus Christ whom Thou hast sent"; and though he had read the words five hundred times before, they came upon him now like a winged message out of heaven. "Blessed be God," he cried, "this word will suffice for all eternity" – and went singing to his death. "There appeared an angel to him strengthening him"; and that word from St. John was the angel.

And today we stand to lose terribly if we leave the Bible out of our reckoning. For right through the pages of this Book runs the frontier-line between two worlds. Here is your listening-post for messages from the beyond. Here messengers of grace move to and fro between one world and the other. Here angels ascend and descend upon the sons of men. A generation that forsakes its Bible is shutting itself off from the eternal world, and depriving itself of indispensable resources for the battle.

> The angels keep their ancient places; –
> Turn but a stone, and start a wing!
> 'Tis ye, 'tis your estranged faces,
> That miss the many-splendoured thing.

But why should we miss it? For whenever a congregation meets, the strengthening angel which is the Word of God is moving in and out amongst them. He is standing now perhaps beside one who has brought with him into God's House some frightful personal worry, and he is saying: "Cast your burden on the Lord." The angel moves on to another who is facing during this coming week some daunting task of critical difficulty, and he says "The Lord is the strength of my life; of whom shall I be afraid?" He is now standing, that angel, beside a third, a young man perhaps who has been losing faith and has almost reached the point of saying – "I don't believe in a spiritual world! I don't believe there is a divine purpose in control. I don't and can't believe!" And like Elisha at Dothan the angel says, "Lord, open his eyes, that he may see." "And the Lord opened the eyes of the young man; and he saw: and behold the mountain was full of horses and chariots of fire." Yes, they are all here, the strengthening angels of the Lord, if only we would take time to meet them – here in this Word of God we too frequently ignore – the angel of pardon, the angel of peace and fortitude, the angel that keeps the gate of heaven.

But there is another form that this experience we are thinking of may take. "There appeared an angel from heaven strengthening him." *Sometimes the strengthening angel is a fellow-creature.* Sometimes it is a friend. It is a fact to which many of us here would bear witness – that one way God has chosen to draw near to us has been through our contact with some human being who had the blessed faculty of turning our weakness into strength, someone to whom today it would be our instinctive tribute: "You have been an angel of God to me!"

When men looked on Stephen as he died, they said his face was like the face of an angel; and there are those who have had that effect upon us by their life – have made us sure that the divine was very near, sure that they had been sent to us by heaven. Silas Marner, in George Eliot's story, finds a little child asleep at his fireside; and from that moment the hard and hopeless heart of the old miser is softened and changed and redeemed. Pippa, in Browning's poem, sings her innocent song along the street, quite unaware of any listeners; and one man, hearing it, is arrested on the very edge and precipice of terrible sin, as though some strong rescuing angel had barred the way. Christian, in Bunyan's allegory, is losing his nerve in the darkest part of the valley, when suddenly from somewhere on ahead of him comes the sound of singing; and the wayfarer of the night, hearing that voice of the unknown traveller on in front of him, the song of another pilgrim of eternity there in the valley beside him, finds his courage reborn and his faith renewed. Thank God for those dear human friends who have brought the reinforcement of heaven into our weak and wavering lives. "There appeared an angel from heaven, strengthening him."

> Then, in such hour of need
> Of your fainting, dispirited race,
> Ye, like angels, appear,
> Radiant with ardour divine.
> Ye fill up the gaps in our files,
> Strengthen the wavering line,
> Stablish, continue our march,
> On, to the bound of the waste,
> On, to the City of God.

If this has been true for you, then don't you think that you in turn might be the strengthening angel for someone else? There is such a mass of trouble in the world; and so many of the people you encounter in the street or your business or your church are fighting a much harder battle and carrying heavier burdens than you might ever guess; and under God it is a Christian privilege to help and cheer them on their way.

Was it not Rabbi Duncan who declared that the character in history whom he envied most, the one he would have asked to be if he could have been given his choice, was the angel of the garden who strengthened Jesus in His agony? But we have our Lord's own word for it that we can indeed be that angel, by helping to lift some other's load, to rally the courage in the depths of some fainting heart. "Inasmuch as ye have done it unto one of the least of these My brethren, ye have done it unto Me."

I have spoken of two ways the angels come to us—through the Word of God, or the personality of a friend. But there is still a third way: for *sometimes the angel is none other than the Lord Himself*. It is Christ who appears to us, to strengthen us. Indeed, in a sense, it is always Christ. When some word from the Bible lays hold of me, it is not just a word out of a Book: it is Christ acting on me through that word. When some friendship reinforces me, it is not just a touch of human kindness: I feel that Jesus of Nazareth has been passing by. And if you would go through this world without weakness or dishonour, there is nothing you ought to pray for more fervently than an acute awareness of the presence of the living Christ.

There was a dark night when the storm was fierce in Galilee and the winds were a howling gale, and the disciples caught in their boat on the loch felt sure they would never live to see the morning. Peering into the dark, they observed something moving swiftly towards them across the waters: at first they imagined it was a spectre, then they thought it was an angel, and then suddenly there was a great shout from Peter – "It's the Master! It's Jesus!" There appeared to them the Lord of angels strengthening them. Some of us would never have been here today if this very thing had not happened to us. Some would have made shipwreck long ago in the stress of trouble or the storm of temptation, if Christ had not been there miraculously at the crucial moment and gripped us with His hand.

Paul in one place bewails his human frailty and impotence. "I am under the law of death," he says in Romans vii, and at great length he elaborates his predicament. "I cannot do what I should. O wretched man that I am, who shall deliver me?" But you turn a single page to Romans viii, and you find him crying victoriously – "There is now no condemnation. I am free from the law of sin and death!" What has happened within the compass of half a page? Simply this – that in between he has met Someone. There appeared unto him a Greater than any angel, strengthening him. "Who shall deliver me? I thank my God," he cries, "Christ will! Christ has delivered me!"

And Paul has no monopoly of that. It is God's free offer through the gospel to us all. And if there is anyone here walking in darkness and having no light, bruised and hurt in spirit, or experiencing a veritable Gethsemane of regret and shame, you can be quite certain that you are not alone: there is Someone there beside you stronger than legions of angels from the realms of glory. He is with you now. For He is here in this church.

> I cannot do without Thee!
>   I cannot stand alone;
> I have no strength nor goodness
>   Nor wisdom of my own.
> But Thou, beloved Saviour,
>   Art all in all to me,
> And perfect strength in weakness
>   Is theirs who lean on Thee.

May that dear strengthening Christ go with you on your pilgrimage; and into the fellowship of the citizens above may the King of angels bring us all.

IO

LIFE'S MOST
INDISPENSABLE POSSESSION

"Take not Thy Holy Spirit from me." — Psalm li. 11.

THAT IS AN abrupt cry from the edge of the abyss. It is the cry of a man suddenly feeling that the foundations of his world are in danger of being swept away. "Take anything else I have, but not the one thing that makes life livable! Take not Thy Holy Spirit from me."

You may call this picture in the psalm overdrawn. You may feel it has very little connection with ourselves, worshipping God here today in tolerable comfort and security. You may think this man's shattering experience is right outside the orbit in which we normally live and move and have our being. We are not crying to God from the edge of any abyss. This is irrelevant.

But wait a moment!

You and I have our faith today — thank God for that! But do we never find ourselves wondering how we should fare if for one reason or another that faith in God were gone and we were left spiritually unsupported? Do we never have moments when we feel that the mounting pressure of life, its frustrations and vexations, its deadly wear and tear, its hard humdrum necessities, are threatening to dim down or even extinguish many a heavenly vision that once cheered us on our way?

When Robert Browning breaks in boisterously, crying:

> Grow old along with me!
> The best is yet to be—

are there not moods in which we want to raise an angry, disbelieving question-mark against that confident philosophy, and tell him bluntly it is not true? St. Paul put it another way. "Though our outward man perish, yet the inward man is renewed day by day." Yes, Paul, it is lovely no doubt when it happens like that. But suppose it does not? Suppose our inward spiritual man is not renewed to match the dwindling of the physical enthusiasm, suppose the inner man goes on dwindling too and the fire of the spirit burns low, what are the prospects then?

You see, this psalmist's cry is not really so strange and unfamiliar after all. At some time most of us have stood or will stand just where he stood then. "Take not Thy Holy Spirit from me."

Now what I want to do is to let the light of the gospel fall upon this text and this experience.

Consider, first, *what it means to possess and to lose the Spirit.* I would put it like this. To be aware of and obedient to the inner voice that speaks in conscience, to be alert and sensitive to the mind of Christ—this is what it is to have the Spirit. To have a faith that takes God at His word, to have a hope that looks beyond the darkness to the dawn, to have a love that sees in every human creature a brother for whom Christ died—this it is to have the Spirit. To be alive to the existence of a world unseen; to realise that the common ways of life are continually being interpenetrated by another dimension, the dimension of the eternal; to have glimpses, even in the here and now, of a supra-human quality of life – this it is to have the Spirit.

> And every virtue we possess,
> And every victory won,
> And every thought of holiness
> Are His alone.

Well may the psalmist cry – "Take not Thy Holy Spirit from me!"

But now look at the other side of it. What does it mean to lose the Spirit?

This. To be unresponsive to the still small voice, insensitive to the living God, and weary of the irksomeness of Christ – this is what it means to lose the Spirit. To grow sceptical about faith, disillusioned about hope, cynical about love – this it is to lose the Spirit. To feel that the struggle between good and evil is not worth the battle; to find your spiritual zest and idealism smothered by the dust and dreariness of life, replaced by moral lassitude and inertia and debility; to stop caring for religion, to find prayer weariness and belief a sham, to record as the final verdict on it all "Vanity and vexation of spirit and a striving wind" – this is to lose the Spirit. Well may any of us cry – "Take not Thy Holy Spirit from me!"

Consider, in the second place, that *thus to lose the Spirit is of all deprivations the most far-reaching and calamitous.* I can illustrate this best by some analogies.

Think, for example, of a musician deprived of the music that is his life. The tragedy of Beethoven was that he went stone-deaf; he never heard, except intellectually, his own greatest melodies. I have visited several times the house in Bonn on the Rhine where Beethoven was born and lived. It is now a museum; and one of the most poignant exhibits is a big glass case full of

116

the strangest ear-trumpets of all shapes and sizes, from an inch or two to two or three feet. This was the composer desperately trying to hear the music he would never hear again. Well might Beethoven have cried – "Take not my music from me!"

Or think of a devotee of Nature being deprived of Nature's beauty. Some of you will remember the scorching, tumultuous words that Bernard Shaw puts into the mouth of Saint Joan when her judges have sentenced her to perpetual imprisonment. Send me to the stake rather than that, she cries. "To shut me from the light of the sky and the sight of fields and flowers; to chain my feet so that I can never again climb the hills – this is worse than the furnace seven times heated. Without these things I cannot live; and by your wanting to take them away from me, I know that your counsel is of the devil, and that mine is of God." So might any devotee of beauty cry – "Take not this fair world of Nature from me!"

Or you might think of an exile deprived of country and home. All exiles in every age speak the same language: whether it is Robert Louis Stevenson far away in the South Seas dreaming of the moors of Scotland –

Blows the wind today, and the sun and the rain are flying,
  Blows the wind on the moors today and now,
Where about the graves of the martyrs the whaups are crying,
  My heart remembers how!

– or whether it is the Hebrew poet of Israel's captivity – "By the rivers of Babylon, there we sat down; yea, we wept, when we remembered Zion. We hanged our harps upon the willows in the midst thereof. How shall we sing the Lord's song in a strange land?" "Take not my country and my home from me!"

Or just once again, you could think of a loving heart deprived by death of the dear object of its love. There are partings that

117

pierce life with pain unspeakable, the aching elemental poignancy of that last farewell, the grief that binds all generations into one, the same yesterday, today and for ever: "O my son Absalom! my son, my son Absalom! Would God I had died for thee, O Absalom, my son, my son!" "Take not my love from me!"

These are analogies. But now this has to be said: desolating as such privations are, the one of which the psalmist speaks is more desolating still. After all, Beethoven could triumph in affliction, and Joan of Arc go through the fire to victory, and exiled Israel lead captivity captive, and love and heartbreak look beyond parting to a wonderful reunion where there shall be no more parting again for ever. As long as you have the Spirit of God, all these other desolations are at least bearable. As long as that Spirit remains, you can see life through with honour. But if once that Spirit should go, then gone is all the reinforcement: no light to guide, no voice to interpret and give meaning, no hand to steady and control. Then indeed is Paradise lost and chaos is come again. This is the last intolerable loneliness. This is life's uttermost of desolation. "Take not Thy Holy Spirit from me."

Consider, in the third place, the question: *But is this risk real?* Can this thing happen? Does God ever remove His Spirit? Would He ever think of taking His Spirit away from anyone?

What of all the texts that say — "I will never leave you nor forsake you. Lo, I am with you always, even unto the end"? Surely the psalmist is imagining the impossible! Surely in this risky world, here is one risk for which we are guaranteed immunity! For surely you cannot conceive God looking out from heaven and seeing some poor unhappy creature stumbling through the dark, and God saying "I am finished with that man! Henceforth I leave him to his own devices." Can that happen? Does God ever take His Spirit away? This is the question.

There was an old Jewish tradition about the final destruction of Jerusalem and its temple by the Roman legions in the great siege of the year A.D. 70. It was said that just before the final assault loud mysterious voices had been heard echoing through the temple, crying "Let us depart!" — and there had been a sound of great unearthly wings sweeping out across the darkening skies; and this was Jehovah and His attendant cherubim and seraphim abandoning the disobedient city to its fate, God finally, withdrawing from the temple that had failed to do Him honour. Legend? No doubt. But what of God's human temples? "Ye are the temple of the Holy Ghost," says the Bible. Is it perhaps not legend there, but fact — the departing Deity, the retreating wings, the irretrievable abandonment?

There is no simple answer to that question. But part at least of the answer would have to be this. There are things in life that certainly break our fellowship with God. They interpose a barrier, and disqualify us for any living awareness of His Spirit.

One is neglect — neglect of prayer, neglect of the faculty of spiritual vision. For neglect of this faculty, as of any faculty, inevitably spells its atrophy and decay. There is one significant, pathetic passage in Charles Darwin's life where the great scientist tells how in his younger days he had loved music and art and literature, having a real faculty for them all and finding intense delight in them; but how latterly he had lost all taste for them, because of his constant one-sided concentration on his scientific calculations. He had in fact reached the point where he could not endure to read a line of poetry and found even Shakespeare nauseatingly dull. "If I had my life to live over again," wrote Darwin, "I would make it a rule to read some poetry and listen to some music at least once every week" — just to keep the faculty alive. So on a deeper level, to neglect the

119

Science can kill the soul. — human dimensions are more than that an

faculty of spiritual vision is to condemn it to a similar degenera-
tion. "Take the talent from him," said the master in Jesus'
parable of the man who would not use his gift, "take it away
from him!" If we will not use our capacity for the Spirit nor
exercise our faculty of faith, we need not hope to keep them.
This is the nemesis of neglect.

But neglect is passive. There is a more active attitude that
tells in the same direction, breaking fellowship and destroying
a man's openness to the divine Spirit – the attitude of rebellion,
the secret revolt, the sin that clouds the soul.

Now this is the clue to the fifty-first psalm, from which our
text is taken. For according to tradition, this psalm was written
by David after the blackest hour of his life. David, shepherd-
king of Israel, had broken the vows which in the day of his
anointing he had made to the high God of his salvation. He had
stolen Bathsheba and sent the brave soldier Uriah to his death.
He – David – had done this. "How art thou fallen from heaven, .
O daystar, son of the morning!" And all these months since, a
restless remorse had been rankling in his heart. He had tried to
pray, and no prayer would come. He had bowed in worship
before the throne of heaven, and God was silent to him and
gave him no sign. And so the dark cloud lowered and the black
mood deepened. And then one day at last Nathan the prophet
had come and with one swift rapier thrust had pierced the king's
defences: "Thou art the man!" And in that instant, as in a
sudden lightning-flash across the darkness, David saw where these
past months of unrepented, unforgiven sin had brought him –
to the verge of a terrible abyss, from which now shuddering he
recoiled.

Martin Luther once on a similar day was heard to cry
beseechingly – "Punish us, O God, punish us, but be not silent
towards us!" For anything is more bearable than that ominous
silence of heaven; any discipline of punishment, any fire of
judgment more tolerable than that fading out of the vision, that

growing dumb of the voice, which are the nemesis of the soul's rebellion. It was with the realisation of how near he had come to being a castaway that David raised beseeching hands to heaven: "Take not Thy Holy Spirit from me!"

Now let us see the point we have reached. We have considered, first, what it means to lose the Spirit; second, the magnitude of this deprivation; and third, its possibility.

But when we have reached this point, suddenly a great burst of gospel light comes breaking from this text. This is the last thing I ask you to consider; and it is the most important of all. *The very fact that the psalmist could make this cry proved that the Spirit was still there.* For, you see, it was precisely God's Spirit within him that made him cry like this. This is in fact an instance of what Paul described to the Romans as "the Spirit Himself making intercession for us with groanings that cannot be uttered."

Here on the day when David miserably felt he had reached rock bottom, he suddenly discovered that he had reached the Rock of Ages. In the moment of his despairing cry "Take not Thy Holy Spirit from me," he was nearer the heart of God than he had been for months. This, I repeat, is the gospel shining through: and it means that when you have touched the depths, you have touched the everlasting arms.

Take any of us here today. How comes it about that we are here? Surely our broken vows, our frequent failures, would long ago have justified God in removing His Spirit from us once for all. And yet – the very fact that we are here in God's House is evidence of His Spirit still operating in our lives. And therefore to the most discomfited soul here today the word of the Lord would be precisely Jesus' word to His disconsolate disciples long ago: "Look up, and lift up your heads, for your redemption has come nigh!"

May I say a special word in closing to anyone whom the

pressure of these days has been victimising? You have had your
share – perhaps more than your share – of the elemental facts of
pain and discipline and trial and loneliness. You have felt faith
strained to the point where it begins breaking down into
unbelief. It may be you have been brought quite near to the
breaking-point, almost (humanly speaking) to the end of your
tether. You have experienced the same forsakenness that the
psalmist knew, and Job and Elijah and Jeremiah. Be of good
courage! For that is precisely the kind of experience that gives
God His best chance. It is far opener to His Spirit than any
amount of glib, facile religious profession.

For once there walked this earth a Man who had not where to
lay His head. In nakedness and pain and desolation He tasted
death for every man, and out of the last darkness cried "My
God, My God, why hast Thou forsaken Me?" And God in
everlasting mercy brought Christ through, and set Him on
high, and shattered death with resurrection; so that today
wherever the name of Jesus is called upon – even if it is only a
half articulate cry, "Jesus, from Your cross have mercy!" – He
is veritably present in the midst. This is not pious metaphor. It
is sober fact.

You may have been having a difficult time in all conscience,
and life may have hurt you sore. But do you not see that it
is just there through the tender mercy of your God that the day-
spring from on high has visited you? And the secret of weather-
ing the storm in the day when the rain descends and the floods
come and the winds blow and beat upon the house – the secret
is not your tenacity and endurance: it is God's constancy, Christ's
fidelity. Place your confidence there, and you build on the rock
that nothing can move.

There was a night many years ago when one of Henry
Drummond's great student meetings in Edinburgh was nearing
its end, and Drummond was appealing for decisions. "I cannot
guarantee," he said, "that the stars will shine brighter when you

LIFE'S MOST INDISPENSABLE POSSESSION

leave this hall tonight, or that when you wake tomorrow a new world will open before you. But I do guarantee that Christ will keep that which you have committed to Him." He will keep His promise, right on to the unknown end.

I should be a fool to stand here today and talk to you about religion, if I were not dead sure of that elemental fact. I know Whom I have believed. I know that His promise stands fast for ever.

> Jesus, my Lord! I know His Name,
>   His Name is all my boast;
> Nor will He put my soul to shame,
>   Nor let my hope be lost.

> I know that safe with Him remains,
>   Protected by His power,
> What I've committed to His trust,
>   Till the decisive hour.

II

WHY GO TO CHURCH

"Ye are come unto mount Sion, and unto the city of the living God, the heavenly Jerusalem, and to an innumerable company of angels, to the general assembly and church of the firstborn, which are written in heaven, and to God the Judge of all, and to the spirits of just men made perfect, and to Jesus the mediator of the new covenant, and to the blood of sprinkling, that speaketh better things than that of Abel. See that ye refuse not him that speaketh."—Hebrews xii. 22–25.

WHAT THIS WRITER is doing is to describe what it felt like in those early generations to belong to the Christian community —and what it ought to feel like to belong to that community still today. He is trying to give some idea of the amazingly rich inheritance which is ours in the Church, the Body of Christ. "When you meet in your places of worship," he says in effect, "with whom are you meeting?" And then he proceeds to tell them. He tells them first negatively, casting his mind back to the old days before God in the fullness of time had sent forth His Son. "You have not come unto the mount that might be touched, and that burned with fire, nor unto blackness, and darkness, and tempest": you have not come, that is, to Sinai, to the voice of thunder that might freeze the blood and terrify the soul; not come to the old rigid system of exclusion, where only Moses could see the face of God, and common sinners had

to keep their distance and tremble in their God-forsakenness –
you have not come to that! All that, having served its day, is
past and finished. And then he goes on to tell them positively.
"You have come to Mount Zion, to myriads of angels in festal
array, to the Church of the firstborn written in heaven, to the
God of all who is Judge, to the spirits of the blessed departed,
and to Jesus and His saving blood." This is your Christian
heritage, declares this man to his readers, and says it still to you
and me; this is the truth about the Church at worship. And
notice precisely how he puts it. He does not say "You shall
come," forecasting something dim and far away, in another
world beyond the grave. He says, "You have come": meaning,
"This is what actually happens every time you meet for worship. This is the fellowship into which you enter." If only we
could realise the riches of our heritage!

It is an amazing wealth of suggestion that this writer has
piled up here in disorderly profusion. Can we get some order out
of it? I think we can. He is saying five things about our fellowship of Christian worship in the Church.

He begins with this: it is *a spiritual fellowship*. "You have come
unto mount Zion, the city of the living God, the heavenly
Jerusalem." "You Christians," he means, "have direct touch
with that invisible spiritual world which is the only ultimate
reality. You are not prisoners behind the bars of a narrow earth-
bound existence, where men push and jostle one another for
their tawdry, perishable prizes, and breathe the suffocating,
poisonous air of a materialist philosophy. You are done with
that! You have had your horizons stretched immeasurably.
You are breathing the ampler air of spiritual truth. You have
come unto mount Zion." For the bedrock reality of the universe
is spiritual.

Let us be clear, however, what this means and what it does
not mean. There is a frequent error we must guard against here.

Far too often the spiritual has been set over against the secular as though these were different realms. This is a complete misunderstanding of the biblical revelation. The spiritual world is emphatically not something apart from the world of mundane affairs and the ordinary workaday life of men. How could it be, seeing that it is precisely in that world and its relationships that God keeps drawing near to us? It is ultimately there we have to find and acknowledge Him, if He is ever to be found at all. Therefore to isolate the sacred from the secular, as is so often done, is thoroughly alien to the intention of the gospel. The final rebuke to such a false division is the incarnation itself, when spirit and matter were for ever united by the fiat of God, and the Word was made flesh.

But now notice: so far from making acts of worship unnecessary, this renders them all the more essential. For we are not likely to go on believing for very long that God is with us in every common task and duty, including the hours when we cannot consciously be thinking of Him at all, unless we make room for times and seasons when we think of Him above everything else, and deliberately "stay our mind upon Him". "All life ought to be worship," declared William Temple; but he went on to add, "We know quite well there is no chance it will be worship unless we have times when we have worship and nothing else."

Now you know, as I know, how this highway of the spirit tends to get blocked by the dust and drudgery of life. The great Indian mystic, Rabindranath Tagore, once wrote a poem in which he compared our daily life to a narrow lane overhung with high buildings, between which there could be seen above a single strip of blue sky torn out of space. The lane, seeing the sun only for a few minutes at midday, asks herself – Is it real? Feeling some wayward breeze of spring wafted in from far-off fields, she asks – Is it real? But the dust and rubbish never rouse her to question. The noise of traffic, the jolting carts, the refuse, the smoke — these she accepts, these she concludes are clearly the real and actual things of life; and as for that strange strip of blue above, she soon ceases even to wonder about it, for so manifestly it is only a fancy, nothing real. This, says Tagore in effect, is precisely the truth about our ordinary mundane existence. The near things, the tangible, material things — these we accept, these we say are obviously the things that matter, they are solid, substantial fact: not recognising that it is that streak of blue above, that far glimpse of the spiritual, which is the essential reality for which every soul of man is made, and which alone gives meaning and perspective to all life's tasks and relationships.

Yes, we forget it; and yet sometimes, thank God, it comes back to haunt us. Sometimes, as Browning knew, "a sunset touch, a fancy from a flower-bell, someone's death" will disturb our too confident security. And specially in the worship of the Church, and above all through the mystery of Holy Communion, the world unseen may break right in upon us. Eternity then stirs within our hearts, and we can doubt the spiritual realities no longer, and we know we are going to be restless until we rest in God. God grant that this may happen every time we come up into His courts. "You have come unto mount Zion, the city of the living God, the heavenly Jerusalem."

I pass to the second fact our text underlines concerning the fellowship of Christian worship: it is *a universal fellowship*. "You have come to the Church of the firstborn, who are written in heaven." The writer is thinking there not of the Church in glory but of the actual Christian society. In other words, this is the magnificent idea of the beloved community. You who belong to Christ, he declares, are no longer isolated and alone. You are members of the greatest fellowship on earth, the Church universal.

Now, of course, it is a great thing to be loyal to one's own congregation, to be able to say that the very stones of the building where you worship week by week are dear to your heart. That is splendid. But do let us remember the greater heritage and the wider horizon! Think of belonging to a fellowship which from its small beginnings in an upper room has grown and extended until today it is as wide as the world. Dead must he be of soul who does not feel the thrill of belonging to a fellowship like that! *My county.*

Faber in one of his hymns complains – "We make God's love too narrow by false limits of our own." He might have said the very same thing about the Church. We make God's Church too narrow by false limits of our own. Too often men have built again with mistaken zeal the very barriers Christ came to level to the dust, racial barriers, class barriers, barriers of sect, denomination and government, of taste and temperament, until the whole fellowship ideal has been pitifully impoverished and restricted. But in the providence of God, such has been the innate vitality of this ideal that not all the excesses of militant nationalism, not all the outbursts of racial bitterness, not all the mad follies of the sectarian spirit, not all the pathetic spiritual exclusiveness which has claimed a monopoly of the grace of God, have ever been quite able to destroy it. It is a tremendous fact, the universal fellowship. Surely it does mean something to us all that the hymns we sing here in church are being sung in Africa, in India, in China, in the islands of the furthest seas. It does mean something that a Kagawa in Japan, a Schweitzer in Africa, a Bonhöffer in Europe, could feel themselves to be blood-brothers in Christ. It does mean something to me to receive, as I did in the days just before the last missionaries had to withdraw from China, a letter from the city of Sian in the province of Shensi, telling me of a great open-air gathering of young Chinese students and others who had come together to listen to half a dozen of their own number speaking of – what do you think? Communism? Nonsense! "What Jesus Christ means to me."

And it does matter mightily that you and I within this church today should know that we are not isolated units brought together by the fact of meeting beneath the same roof or belonging to one congregation, but that outside these walls there is a great unnumbered host worshipping the same Lord Christ, feeling towards Jesus just as we feel towards Him, thanking God for Jesus just as we thank God for Him, pledged to stand up and fight for Jesus just as we are pledged to stand up and fight for Him.

There is no other fellowship – social, political or international – which can compare for a moment with this. Some of you may remember those dreadful militaristic demonstrations which we could hear broadcast from Europe occasionally before the war, thousands of voices shouting fanatically *"Sieg, Heil!"* – yelling it in menacing unison, *"Sieg, Heil"!* There is a louder chorus than that across the world today, if only we were able to hear it. And if I could stand in this pulpit and shout the words "Christ is risen" across the thousands of miles to Nigeria, Uganda, Bengal, Manchuria, Brazil, Jamaica, back would come the cry, drowning all other sounds, "Yes, He is risen indeed! Hallelujah!"

It is an incomparable thing, this universal fellowship. And every time you come to church, says this writer to the Hebrews, this is the fellowship you enter. "You have come to the Church of the firstborn, who are written in heaven."

I pass to the third description he gives of our fellowship in Christian worship. It is *an immortal fellowship.* "You have come to myriads of angels in festal array, and to the spirits of just men made perfect." He is away now, you see, across the river in the Church invisible and triumphant. He is away in that other world where all the celestial hosts sing to the Lord, ten thousand times ten thousand uniting in the great Te Deum of heaven: "Worthy is the Lamb that was slain to receive power, and riches, and wisdom, and strength, and honour, and glory, and blessing." And what he says is immensely important for all of us who here on earth have had to face the sorrow of separation, all for whom the poet in his bereavement spoke:

> Thy voice is on the rolling air;
> I hear thee where the waters run;
> Thou standest in the rising sun,
> And in the setting thou art fair.

For what this writer says to us is this: "When you Christians are at worship, bowing in prayer before the throne on high, then your loved ones on the other side are very near to you, and the cloud of witnesses is all round about you. In coming to commune with the world unseen, you are come to the spirits of just men made perfect – the immortal fellowship."

There is a lovely old Greek play, the *Alcestis* of Euripides, which tells how the hero Heracles, the Samson of the Greeks, once met and conquered death. There was a day when Heracles on a journey came to the palace of King Admetus; and there he found everyone desolate with grief because Death, that bitter tyrant, had carried off the fair young Queen Alcestis. Whereupon Heracles, who in his day had fought and tamed many wild beasts and dangerous monsters, the lion and the bull, the Hydra and Cerberus, offered to go out to the grave and face this last grim enemy and rob him of his prize. Away out to the lonely tomb he went; and there he met the monster Death, and grappled with him and vanquished him, and set his victim free. And the most beautiful scene in the drama is that in which Heracles comes leading by the hand someone completely covered with a white veil, and stands before the heartbroken King, and cries –

> Look on her, if in aught she seems to thee
> Like to thy wife. Step forth from grief to bliss.

130

And he lifts the veil, and there is Alcestis, alive and fair and smiling as of old. "See, O King, I give her back to thee." Of course the Greeks knew that it was myth and fable. That kind of thing does not happen in this world. But come across into Christianity, and it is no myth nor fable now. A greater than Heracles is here. Our Master has met the last enemy and vanquished it for ever: so that today from across the river there comes, blown back to you, the sound of singing:

> Ev'n as a bird
>   Out of the fowler's snare
> Escapes away,
>   So is our soul set free:
> Broke are their nets,
>   And thus escaped we.

"See," says Christ to you whom death has robbed, "I give him back — I give her back — to you!" And with that, you know that your loved one is alive for ever and intimately near you still.

No, they are not far away, the spirits of just men made perfect; and those who love God never meet for the last time. They are still watching over us who are left journeying and battling here, still rallying our faint hearts to cheer us on our way. It is said that when Napoleon with his Grand Army was crossing the Alps the troops at one point began to mutiny, refusing to march further, giving up the whole adventure in despair, beaten by the cold and the toilsomeness of that frightful journey. But someone suddenly had an idea: why should the band not play the Marseillaise? As soon as the notes of that thrilling, jubilant melody were heard, there in the wilds of the Alps, the light flashed back into listless eyes, and the strength returned to weary limbs, and they went on and breasted the summits and turned defeat to victory. So our dear ones, from where they dwell with Christ in glory, still cheer and urge us on;

131

and every echo of the new song they sing is a thing to bring the light to our eyes and strength to our fainting hearts. And remember, says this writer to the Hebrews, when you come together for worship they are very near to you then. It is just as if they were holding Christ's right hand, and you His left. They are as near to you as that. "You are come to the spirits of just men made perfect" — the immortal fellowship.

Fourth, it is *a divine fellowship*. "You have come to the God of all who is Judge, and to Jesus the Mediator of the new covenant." In your worship, he tells them, reaching now the very heart of the matter, you have come to God as revealed in Jesus. And, indeed, without this all the other great things he has spoken of would be insufficient and unavailing. But beyond all these, he now says, deeper than all these, you have come right through to Christ.

It is said that a friend of Leonardo da Vinci's, looking at the unfinished picture of the Last Supper, was entranced by the loveliness of two silver cups on the table in front of Jesus, and immediately exclaimed at the artistic skill of their design. Leonardo's retort was to take his brush and paint them out. "It is not that I want you to see," he exclaimed, "it is that Face!" And is there anything we need to see but just that face of Jesus?

For never a congregation meets for worship but some are present perplexed and baffled and oppressed by the difficult problems of life; and the inarticulate longing of their hearts is — "Sir, we would see Jesus." Are there indeed any of us exempt from this experience? Somewhere, we feel sure, there must be a solution to the vexing enigmas of our life, somewhere a transfiguring light across all its meaningless frustrations, somewhere an interpretation of all the discipline we have to bear. And no mere philosophy of life is adequate, no stoic abstract view can finally avail. It is a divine heart we want to speak to, a

Friend who will understand, a living love on which we may confidently lean. "Sir, we would see Jesus."

There is a characteristic little story which is told about Dr. John Duncan. He was scholar, mystic, theologian. He knew the Hebrew language like his mother tongue. It was rumoured among his students that when "Rabbi" Duncan said his prayers at night he prayed to God in Hebrew. One day two of them resolved to listen outside his door at the time of prayer: they would hear those flights of mysticism and theology going up to God in the Hebrew tongue. They listened, and this is what they heard:

> Gentle Jesus, meek and mild,
> Look upon a little child,
> Pity my simplicity,
> Suffer me to come to Thee.

There is nothing deeper than that. We would see Jesus. We are all one in this critical, final need. Suffer me to come to Thee!

And those happy souls who do in fact discover Christ — how different life looks to them! You know the kind of testimony they can bear. "I was battered by trouble, and Christ was my strength and stay. I was lost and groping, and Christ was my guiding light. I have trembled in the fierce fury of the storm, and Christ came to me over the waves and held me up, delivering my soul from death and turning the tempest into calm." This is the testimony.

When the earthquake broke on Philippi, and the prison walls were shaken and the doors burst open, and the gaoler rushed in on Paul and Silas, crying "What shall I do?" — I do not read that the apostles answered, "Run, man, for you life! Quick, before the walls crush you!" What they did say — and the words ring like a trumpet — was "Believe on the Lord Jesus Christ and thou shalt be saved." This is our deepest need. "If there be

one of you," cried a Covenanting preacher to his flock dis-
persing across the moors when the approach of the enemy was
signalled, "if there be one of you, He will be the second. If there
be two of you, He will be the third. You will never, never lack
for company." And every time you come to worship, says this
writer to the Hebrews, you can be quite certain you are coming
to Jesus. Do you think any of us could stay away from church
if we realised that?

One other fact about our fellowship in worship he adds, and
so makes an end: it is *a redeeming fellowship*. "You have come to
the blood of sprinkling, that speaketh better things than that of
Abel." For when all is said and done, it is sin that is the trouble.
It is these weak-willed, wayward hearts of ours that are so
desperately undependable. It is not only the stubborn sway of the
sins of the flesh: it is even more the satanic subtlety of the sins
of the spirit, which make us amid all our religious profession so
terribly unlike Jesus — the pride of intellect patronising simpler
folk, the pride of judgment imputing motives, the pride of
religious life making us feel that we are doing rather creditably
and certainly a good deal better than many others. It is these
things that make our very virtues shabby and our righteousnesses like filthy rags; it is these which, when we come alive to
them, may well reduce us to despair, as we realise the devastating truth that even at our best we are bankrupt utterly, and that
all we have ever done or can do is nothing.

But, says this man, "you have come to the blood of sprinkling." Where should any of us be if that were not true? If
Christianity were not above everything else a religion of redemption?

And, he goes on, it "speaketh better things than that of
Abel", or as it might more accurately be translated, "it cries
louder than that of Abel". "The voice of thy brother's blood,"
said God to Cain in the old story, "crieth unto Me from the

ground"; our secret sins, our frequent defeats, go crying up to
God in heaven. If this were all, hope would be gone, and we
could never lift our heads again. But here enters the gospel. For
when our sins cry out to God for punishment and vengeance,
something else also happens, declares this writer to the Hebrews: the blood of Christ cries louder, overbears and drowns
and silences the very crying of our sins, and God for Christ's
sake forgives.

There is a moving scene in Ian Maclaren's *Bonnie Brier Bush,*
where the old country doctor MacLure, who for more than
forty years had been a familiar and well-loved figure in the glen
where he had gone his rounds, has come himself at last to the
end of the day. Beside him in the gloaming there sits his friend
the farmer Drumsheugh. The dying man asks him to read aloud
to him out of the old Book; and Drumsheugh opens the Bible at
the fourteenth of St. John. "Ma mither aye wantit this read tae
her when she was weak." But MacLure stopped him. "It's a
bonnie word, but it's no for the like o' me. It's ower gude; a'
daurna tak it. Shut the buik an' let it open itsel." The farmer
obeyed. He shut the book, and it opened of itself at a much
thumbed page—the story of the penitent sinner in the temple
who "would not lift up so much as his eyes to heaven"—and
through his tears he read these words: "God be merciful to me
a sinner."

And whoever we are, and whatever we are—minister, elder,
deacon, church member, social worker—we all come to that at
last. God be merciful to me a sinner. And the only question that
ultimately matters is, Can God be merciful to such a one as I
am, who must have wearied His mercy so often? Can His
patience indeed hold out to the end? Let me answer it, not in
my own words, but in words that have gone on singing their
way down three hundred years from the Elizabethan age, since
first they were written by John Donne, Dean of St. Paul's, in his
Hymn to God the Father:

Wilt Thou forgive that sin where I begun,
　　Which was my sin, though it were done before?
Wilt Thou forgive that sin, through which I run,
　　And do run still, though still I do deplore?
　　　　When Thou hast done, Thou hast not done,
　　　　　　For I have more.

Wilt Thou forgive that sin which I have won
　　Others to sin, and made my sin their door?
Wilt Thou forgive that sin which I did shun
　　A year or two, but wallowed in, a score?
　　　　When Thou hast done, Thou hast not done,
　　　　　　For I have more.

I have a sin of fear, that when I have spun
　　My last thread, I shall perish on the shore;
But swear by Thyself, that at my death Thy Son
　　Shall shine as He shines now, and heretofore;
　　　　And having done that, Thou hast done,
　　　　　　I fear no more.

And every time you come to church, says this man, you are coming to the blood of sprinkling, that forgives — everything. Everything!

"See that ye refuse not Him that speaketh."

12

OK lovely

MY TIMES ARE IN THY HAND

"The word which came to Jeremiah from the Lord, saying, Arise, and go down to the potter's house, and there I will cause thee to hear my words. Then I went down to the potter's house, and, behold, he wrought a work on the wheels. And the vessel that he made of clay was marred in the hand of the potter; so he made it again another vessel, as seemed good to the potter to make it. Then the word of the Lord came to me, saying, O house of Israel, cannot I do with you as this potter? saith the Lord. Behold, as the clay is in the potter's hand, so are ye in mine hand, O house of Israel." —Jeremiah xviii. 1-6.

IT WAS A perfectly familiar sight. Jeremiah had seen it scores of times. But today it suddenly arrested him, smote him like a revelation.

What was this thing he saw? The apparatus of the potter's trade was simple. It consisted of two large circular stones shaped like wheels, placed horizontally one above the other some distance apart, and joined through the middle by a vertical connecting-rod. The lower stone was kept revolving by the craftsman's feet. This turned the upper stone, on which rested the moist, plastic clay; and there on that whirling surface, with deft touch and practised skill, the potter moulded his vessel.

On this particular occasion when Jeremiah was a spectator, something went wrong. The potter was not satisfied with his work. The vase he was designing turned out not quite

137

symmetrical – perhaps owing to some flaw in the material, some refractory quality in the clay. And Jeremiah was intensely interested in what happened next. The man did not set the imperfect article aside or throw it away. The clay was still soft and pliable; so he crushed it back into a shapeless lump, and started all over again, remoulding it on his wheel. And this time his patience was rewarded by a vase of perfect form and symmetry. So he placed it in the furnace, to fire and harden it, and it came out a thing of usefulness and beauty.

It was then, suddenly, that the prophet saw why he had been led there that day. The swift dramatic analogy flashed upon him. God was the potter, Israel the clay; and the vicissitudes of history were the implements – the wheel, the file, the furnace – by which the divine Craftsman was moulding the national soul. But what patience this Artificer needed! How often this raw material, the soul of Israel, proved perverse and recalcitrant! Throw the wretched, useless thing away! – that would have been natural. But no. Always the divine Craftsman would start again from the beginning. God would not fail nor be discouraged till His purpose was complete.

This, then, was the lesson Jeremiah learned, standing there in the potter's workshop in Jerusalem; and for us today it is immensely apposite. I know, of course, that this analogy – God the potter, ourselves the clay – has its limitations, and it would be risky to press the metaphor too far. For one thing, the clay does not possess free will: we do. The clay cannot consciously oppose the craftsman's design: we can. The clay is not aware of the feel of the potter's hand: we are. So you must not overdrive a metaphor like this. Yet, properly handled, the analogy is valid, graphic, meaningful – relevant to our situation in the highest degree.

Consider, then, some cogent facts which, implicit in Jeremiah's picture, have been made explicit in the Christian gospel.

138

The first thing that meets me here is *the recognition of a dependence:* man's utter dependence upon God. "O house of Israel, cannot I do with you as this potter? saith the Lord."

This indeed, whatever the sceptic may say, is the basic truth of existence. There is a modern scepticism which claims to have demolished God, and abrogated the supernatural, and reduced religion to the level of a Freudian illusion. But man in his deep heart knows better. It is the eternal God who has made us, not we ourselves. He is the Creator, we the creatures; He the potter, we the work of His hands. And all the twentieth-century's technological achievements and man's proud mastery of the universe have not changed that situation by one iota.

Is this not written right through the teaching of Jesus in the Gospels? The whole burden of Jesus' teaching is that it is on God for every breath we depend. It is God's will that brought the universe into being, and holds it together: so that if God were for one moment to withdraw His hand, the whole creation would disintegrate and crash in ruin and cease to be. We are not the architects of destiny. We are not the creators or redeemers of the world. We are God's raw materials. "There's a divinity that shapes our ends." It is God's grace, said R. L. Stevenson, that "makes the nails and axles of the universe." The recognition of a dependence!

Now since this is the basic fact of existence, it follows that human pride, human self-sufficiency, is the basic sin. The nation whose ultimate trust is in its own power and resources; the scientific humanism whose final confidence is in itself; the righteous man who regards his righteous deeds as meritorious and creditable and self-justifying; the Church that regards itself as a miniature Kingdom of God — all are guilty of the one fundamental sin of which all other sins are but derivatives.

After all, what would you think of a poor dauber who should set his amateurish artistic efforts alongside the masterpieces of a Raphael or a Titian and say complacently, "Yes, it's rather good, that work of mine"? What are all our vaunted virtues and achievements alongside the holiness, the almightiness, of God, all our pathetic attainments in the light of the infinite nobility of Christ? It is so ludicrously naïve, this shattering self-sufficiency. The Bible in its usual blunt devastating way has nailed it down by saying that all our righteousnesses are as filthy rags — that every mouth may be stopped before God.

There, then, is one fact in this picture of the potter and his clay — the recognition of a dependence, man's utter dependence upon God. "*Non nobis, Domine*" — this is the cry of the ages — "not unto us, Lord, not unto us, but to Thy name be the glory!"

Pass to a second fact that emerges here. First, the recognition of a dependence: second, *the revelation of a design*. The potter whom Jeremiah saw was not working at random: he was working with a purpose. He had the pattern of the finished product in his mind. Out of the common clay he was fashioning something serviceable, a vessel to be used. That, saw Jeremiah, was God's intention with Israel.

Is it not a marvellously inspiring thought that God has a plan for every one of us? That He is not working at random in the shaping of your life and mine — He is working with a purpose? The revelation of a design!

And mark you, that is true even in the bitter moments when we feel inclined flatly to deny it. "What's the use of my life in the total scheme of things?" we sometimes wonder. "Would it make a scrap of difference if I were not here at all? If I died tonight, there would not be a ripple on the surface of the universe. Where is there any trace of planned and rational pattern giving my life history significance, cohesion and momentum? Design? What nonsense! I don't believe it."

It is when I am tempted to talk like that that there suddenly comes back to me the loving and reproachful voice of Jesus Christ. "Friend," He says, "have faith in God! Trust the divine

Craftsman at His work. He knows what He is doing. God sees eternal possibilities in that soul of yours. He is working out His deep, deliberate design."

> Leave to His sovereign sway
> To choose and to command;
> So shalt thou, wondering, own His way,
> How wise, how strong His hand.

Pass on to another fact that meets us here. The recognition of a dependence, the revelation of a design; and third, *the reason of a discipline.*

For as Jeremiah looked at the harsh implements of the potter's trade — the whirling wheel, the file, the chisel, and the scorching fire — he suddenly saw "That is how God makes men! That is how God is making Israel. That is the cost of the fashioning of character, national and individual." And surely he was right. It is God's implements of discipline and hardship, chastisement and affliction, that grind character into shape. "Oh," cried Samuel Rutherford, "what I owe to the file, and the hammer, and the furnace of my Lord Jesus!" The cost of the fashioning of personality. The reason of a discipline!

Now I wonder if, in the light of this, you would agree with me that our common use of the word "providential" is far too limited and narrow? When we use the word providential, it is generally miraculous deliverances from trouble we are thinking of, eleventh hour escapes, dramatic answers to prayer. "Oh," we say, describing some such experience, "it was simply providential!" And so no doubt it was.

> Ev'n as a bird
>   Out of the fowler's snare
> Escapes away,
>   So is our soul set free.

That is providential. Yes, but ought we really to limit the word like that? Is it only these amazingly good things that are providential? What about the times when we prayed for deliverance, and no deliverance came, the dangers we did not escape, the burdens that were not eased? Are we to see no providence there?

Paul prayed to be delivered from the thorn in his flesh; and if in the twinkling of an eye it had been removed, of course we should have said "How absolutely providential!" Actually it was not removed; to the end of his life it remained; but Paul, seeing deeper than the rest of us into the mysteries of God, said that its non-removal was providential, incomparably profitable for his Christian discipleship.

And must we not say that if the implements of the divine Artificer are the wheel and the chisel and the fire; if these are the means for the moulding of the raw materials and the earthly clay into something serviceable that Christ can use – then we ought to rethink and widen our whole conception of providence? "Whom the Lord loveth He chasteneth, and scourgeth every son whom He receiveth." The reason of a discipline! "Just and true are all Thy ways, Thou King of saints!"

But now, there is a fourth fact that meets us here: *the repudiation of a destiny.* Jeremiah saw that men may use their freedom to repudiate the divine purpose. "The vessel that he made of clay was marred in the hand of the potter." The design miscarried. And this, Jeremiah saw, was his nation's story. How Israel had failed and frustrated God!

So it is today, internationally, when nations turn from the ideals of goodwill and co-operation to the paths of violence and aggression. So it is also, ethically, when a culture, a generation, under the influence of men of trivial mind and dingy morals, proceeds to dissolve the absolute demands of God in a morass of moral relativism, declaring that there are no absolute standards universally valid, and nothing can always be labelled as wrong, and man is free to do as he likes, and it is society that makes the rules: all of which may sound like up-to-date psychology, but is actually sophisticated nonsense. And so it is also, individually, when our own sinful nature reasserts itself, and we rebel against the Hand that guides and the Heart that plans. Our innate self-will – this is the flaw that frustrates so irresponsibly the great Artificer's design: and the vessel is marred, and you have one more tragedy of "what might have been." The repudiation of a destiny!

But that is not the final word. There is a fifth truth that emerges from Jeremiah's picture: and this is *the record of a determination*. Is there any greater parable in Scripture of the indomitable patience of God? For see what the potter did. He might have thrown that faulty vessel away. He might have said "This clay is bad: I can make nothing of it. I must get a fresh supply." But what struck Jeremiah, and what made this incident into a gospel for him, was that the potter did nothing of the kind. He started all over again with the same material. He gathered up the fragments. He pressed the clay into a lump. He placed it on the wheel once more. He told himself "I can, I must, I will make something fine and noble of this yet!" And he did. The record of a determination!

And that, says Jeremiah, is God. That is Israel's everlasting hope. And indeed the whole Bible is a commentary on this divine indomitable patience of the Lord who made us and redeemed us. Why was Jacob not cast out on the scrap-heap for his warped and twisted ways? Why was David not disowned by heaven for the dark degrading deed that made his name a byword in the land? Why was not Peter left to sink after his base denial? Why was not Saul of Tarsus – persecutor, blasphemer, hater of Christ – blotted out from the book of life for ever? Why? Because there is nothing in heaven or earth so dogged and

determined and stubborn and persistent as the grace that wills
to save!

Where should any of us be today if it were not for the infinite
patience of heaven? The logic of life says – "O God, You ought
to have despaired of us long ago. You ought to have left us to
our own devices. You ought, seeing our monotonous defeats at
the hands of temptation, our shoddy pacts and compromises
with evil, our spiritual unreliability and the corruption of our
wills, You ought to have swept us out of Your sight, and
abandoned such intractable, perverse clay as quite useless for
Your purpose." That is what ought to have happened.

Why, then, has it not? Why is it that we can still feel the
hand of the divine Craftsman working – tenderly, indomitably
– in the secret places of our lives? Why are we still visited,
earth-bound creatures as we are, by voices out of the unseen and
the eternal? And why, for all our headlong flight down laby-
rinths of self and sin, why does Christ still pursue us, till He
tracks us down at last? It is the eternal patience in action for
our redeeming. It is the record of a determination. "If I make
my bed in hell, behold, Thou art there!"

One final fact emerges from Jeremiah's picture. Beyond this
record of a determination, there comes *the retrieval of a defeat*.
And the divine strategy here is very wonderful, more wonderful
than some of us have ever understood. It is this: God can work
our very mistakes into the final pattern of His love. When the
first vessel was marred, says Jeremiah, the potter "made it again
another vessel". This time, it would seem, some details of the
pattern were changed. In view of what had happened before,
some alteration had to be introduced into the original plan,
certain features left out, new features incorporated; but in the
end the finished work came forth a thing of beauty. The retrieval
of defeat!

Is there not a great gospel here? God is so wonderful in His grace that He can actually take our very mistakes and blunders, our false choices and wrong turnings, the negative things we should say had ruined the pattern of our life for ever, He can take these and overrule them, using them positively and creatively, working them into the completed design.

That does not mean that our mistakes and sins are excusable and not serious. But it does mean that the grace of God is far more wonderful than some of us have yet envisaged, far more resourceful and inventive. For you see, it means that to the person who believes in God there is no such thing as an irreparable disaster, no discord that cannot contribute to the final harmony, no thorns that cannot be woven into a crown, no breakaway from the original pattern that cannot itself be wrought in by God's skilful fingers to a new completed design.

The Bible does not condone David's frightful blunder that earned him the prophetic accusation "Thou art the man." But it takes that tragic event and works it into the final pattern, in the immortal loveliness and converting power of the great penitential psalms to which that sin gave birth. The Bible does not condone Saul's share in the death of Stephen. But it takes that dark regretted deed and works it into the ultimate design, in the form of Paul's consuming passion for souls. God does not condone the bitter policies that deny His will and drown the world in blood. But in the end—make no mistake—in the end even the wrath and folly of man shall praise Him, and all life's most desperate contradictions shall be compelled to subserve His purpose and not the devil's.

God is not defeated by the sins of men. It is to assure us of this that there stands at the heart of our holy faith a cross. Did God condone that blackest, most colossal deed of man's malignity—the crucifying of Jesus of Nazareth? No! God did not condone the cross. But God took it, and wrought it into His final design, which was and is the saving of the world.

May I in these closing words speak to someone who feels that he or she has missed the mark, and taken the wrong turning, and blundered the pattern of life? What I would say is – Lift up your heart! God's grace can take that point of error where the plan went wrong, and use it and transfigure it, so that the resultant pattern will have an unexpected loveliness of its own and even shine with beauty. This is the retrieval of defeat: and to those who open their hearts in faith it is no wish-thinking or imagination, it is solid, magnificent fact.

Do you know Robert Browning's lines about the divine Artificer and His shaping of our lives?

> So, take and use Thy work:
> Amend what flaws may lurk,
> What strain o' the stuff, what warpings past the aim!
> My times be in Thy hand!
> Perfect the cup as plann'd!
> Let age approve of youth, and death complete the same!

It can happen. But it can happen only to those who open their hearts in faith. Will you do that today? It could make such a mighty difference. For the hands of the great Potter are feeling, feeling for us now. Perhaps some can sense their touch at this moment. And they are such eager, skilful, loving hands, those pierced hands of the divine Craftsman, so eager to take all our human blunderings and confusions, strains and stresses, flaws and warpings and defeats, to take and work these into the final symmetry of His complete and perfect will. My times are in Thy hand! Perfect the cup as planned. And to God be all the glory.

13

ON MEETING TROUBLE
TRIUMPHANTLY

"Blessed be God, even the Father of our Lord Jesus Christ, the
Father of mercies, and the God of all comfort; Who comforteth
us in all our tribulation, that we may be able to comfort them
which are in any trouble, by the comfort wherewith we ourselves
are comforted of God."—2 Corinthians i. 3, 4.

YOU WILL NOTICE that Paul in this sentence uses one word
five times over. That is not deficient vocabulary nor poverty of
literary expression. The fivefold repetition is deliberate. "Here,"
he means, "is a fact which it is quite impossible to overemphasise.
Here is one of the biggest and best authenticated of discoveries.
Here is something which can stand up to the colossal strain of
life and the fierce severity of death." That is why, in this
shining trumpet-toned doxology, he takes the word "comfort"
and rings it out five times over. "Blessed be God, the Father of
our Lord Jesus Christ, the Father of mercies and the God of all
comfort; Who comforteth us in all our tribulation, that we may
be able to comfort them which are in any trouble, by the comfort wherewith we ourselves are comforted of God."

There speaks the voice of personal experience. This is auto-
biography, straight from life. This man is not spinning airy
theories nor weaving pleasant fantasies: he is narrating events,

147

and his logic is hard as nails. He is not looking at the map of a wonderful country in which he has never set foot: he is living in it. So much of our religion is looking at a map, not living in the land. But Paul is different. He is there. He knows.

Thomas Carlyle once, describing his history of the French Revolution, declared — "This I can tell the world, that not for a hundred years have you had a book which has come so direct and flaming from the heart of a living man." That is emphatically true of these words of Paul to the Corinthians: direct and flaming from the heart.

And if ever a man had a right to speak on this theme, Paul surely had that right. For no sheltered life was his. What with shipwreck and stoning, flogging and imprisonment, ill-health and opposition, the misunderstanding of friends and the diabolical devices of vindictive foes, it was a life whose sheer atrocious discomfort appals the imagination. I reckon that if how to manage trouble triumphantly is the theme this is the kind of man we should want to listen to. Paul has earned the right to speak.

So let us listen to him now. You will find, if you ponder these words, that what he is doing is to stress certain vital elements which make Christian comfort what it is.

First, *the distinctive character it displays.* Right at the outset we must be clear what Paul means by this word. It is certainly not what we often mean. You hear people talking about a comfortable income, a comfortable home, sometimes even a comfortable church. The trouble is that our word "comfort" has come down in the world. It has been weakened, cheapened and sentimentalised — so much so that to speak in the same breath of religion and comfort makes some good people squirm. "Can't you see," they would exclaim, "you are playing right into the hands of the sceptic who stigmatises religion as a sentimental escapism?"

So we have to be careful. Certainly there is a way of trying to comfort that is weak and enervating and sentimental. It blurs the moral issues, turns religion into a cushion against the hard facts of life, employs the drug of fantasy. It camouflages the cross, and romanticises the tragic element in life. It uses consolatory phrases to hypnotise the troubled mind into a condition of torpid tranquillity. The comforts of belief and faith are treated as a kind of spiritual medicine, the peace of God as the perfect tranquilliser.

But this coddling, vapid comfort does not even remotely resemble what Paul is talking about here. His word is one of the most virile, non-sentimental words in the New Testament. It is *paraklesis* – and that means "calling in to help". It means the summons that brings reinforcements marching to your aid. Our Authorised Version speaks of the Holy Ghost as the "Comforter". It is the same root. It is the cognate word *parakletos* – as in the hymn, "Come, Thou Holy Paraclete" – and it means the heavenly reinforcement summoned to your side. The corresponding word in Latin is *advocatus*, the counsel for the defence who in the day of trial stands forth as your champion: and this is how our English version actually translates St. John's Paraclete in the great phrase, "We have an Advocate with the Father." So whenever Scripture speaks of the Holy Spirit as the Paraclete or the Comforter, it is not just the Consoler that is meant. Rather is it the Reinforcer, the Strengthener, the Giver of power and might and victory.

In its origins, of course, our English word "comfort" meant the same. For it is just the Latin *con-* and *fortis*, denoting an accession of strength. This, then, is the distinguishing thing about Christian comfort – its bracing, rallying, invigorating quality. When Paul talks here about being comforted, he means having his total personality supernaturally reinforced. Nothing weak or debilitating about this kind of comfort! It is active, virile and indomitable. Its function is, not to equip you with blinkers against disquieting facts, but to arm you in the panoply of God, and so make you adequate to life. It replenishes your spent resources. It works a spiritual renovation. It floods your being with radiance and resilience. This comfort is lyrical with the music of victory, and strong with the omnipotence of God.

Notice, second, *the divine source from which it springs.* "Blessed be God, the Father of mercies and God of all comfort." Paul's profound insight taught him that only the measureless mercy of heaven could avail for the multiple miseries of earth. God of all comfort!

Men have always tried other sources. Perhaps some of us are looking to other sources today.

Some there are, for example, who look for comfort to scientific technology — as though a day would come when all the ills of life, its frictions, stresses and frustrations, would be charmed away and vanish like a troubled dream before the gleaming daybreak of the multifarious miraculous inventions of a scientifically awakened world. Vain hope indeed!

Others again of a different temperament have gone seeking comfort in Nature's vast and varied world. Far be it from me to decry this quest. For I know the strengthening of soul there is in the stillness of a Highland moor or mountain, the beauty of the heather round a Highland loch. But if you trust to Nature, she may fail you; for often she is apt simply to reflect the mood you bring to her, to give you back the joy or sorrow through which you view her. Sometimes her very beauty can hurt rather than heal the soul:

> Ye banks and braes o' bonnie Doon
> How can ye blume sae fair!
> How can ye chant, ye little birds,
> And I sae fu' o' care!

Others again have looked for comfort to psychological suggestion. "Every day and in every way I am getting better and better." Say the words often enough, and with sufficient injection of confidence, and you will be bound to achieve (so it is said) a satisfactory readjustment, with all the peace and poise and comfort you can desire: you will in fact "work out your own salvation". About such utopian optimism the only thing that needs to be said is that it is too naïve and callow to be true.

Others again of a different temperament have looked for comfort amid the troubles of life to the practice of a stoic philosophy. And indeed there is real nobility here. Resolutely the stoic sets himself to be master of his fate and captain of his soul and architect of his destiny. Self-control, self-sufficiency, self-determination — these are his watchwords. "Soul of mine," he says, "play the man! No flinching! No surrender to emotion! No giving in to weakness! Your will is unconquerable, if you choose to have it so. Hold the fort, crush down your feelings, defy the devilries of fate, and you win a peace inviolable for ever." This is stoic comfort. Valiant? Yes. Don't dare to minimise its valour. And yet — were I to offer this as a gospel, would it not be an empty mockery, a monstrous contradiction? Vanity of vanities indeed!

Others again have gone to the opposite extreme and sought the comfort of a hedonistic ethic. "Let us eat, drink and be merry," says the cheerful modern pagan, "let us not scruple overmuch about rights and wrongs which are in any case mainly taboos and conventions. The secret of a comfortable existence is the ability to relax." That blessed word "relax"! So often, as used today, it means simply to drift into secularism, materialism, self-absorption. No comfort there! That creed becomes like Dead Sea fruit in the mouth.

So we come round again to the apostle and to his great discovery: "Blessed be God, Father of mercies and God of all comfort!" There had been a time when Paul himself had tried to find comfort elsewhere – in pride of nationality, righteousness of life, blamelessness of conscience; and the more he had tried, the more desperately uncomfortable he had grown. But the day when he met Christ, the day when he had opened his heart to Christ and caught something of Christ's Spirit, that day the comfort and the peace of God entered into him and possessed him, became so real and pervasive that never from that moment were the thousand vicissitudes of his life able to dislodge it.

> Let me no more my comfort draw
> From my frail hold on Thee;
> In this alone rejoice with awe,
> Thy mighty grasp of me!

This, then, is what the revelation of God in Christ has given us: the feel of a divine Hand upon our life – "Thy mighty grasp of me" – the healing power of the dimension of eternity, the reassuring music of the promise "I will not leave you comfortless, I will come to you". This is not dead dogma I am telling you: it is life-transforming truth, verifiable by anyone today. This is the comfort of the Lord.

We have seen the divine source from which it springs, and the distinctive character it displays. The third fact Paul stresses is *the illimitable range it covers*. "Blessed be God, who comforteth us in all our tribulation," in all our troubles of every kind. There is no conceivable situation to which it does not apply. Paul himself had tested it thoroughly. Think of the four major species of trouble to which human nature is heir. Paul knew them all.

Physical trouble. This man had his "thorn in the flesh", his recurring, frustrating bouts of crippling illness. He knew from repeated experience the indescribable squalor of oriental gaols.

He was stoned by the mobs, flogged by the lashes of the Roman police. That is what he means when he reminds the Galatians, "I bear in my body the marks of the Lord Jesus." And through it all – "My grace is sufficient for thee!" At midnight in the dungeon at Philippi he and Silas could sing aloud for joy, so that the other prisoners heard them. "He comforteth us in all our physical trouble."

Yes, and mental trouble too – the pressure of anxiety. Paul knew the anxious care of being a father in God to all sorts and conditions of people, the frightful worry of seeing young churches corrupted into heresy and young converts relapsing into paganism, the constant, wearing concern for the whole future of the work. He calls it in one place "the care of all the churches". And through it all he found, he says, that "the peace of God would stand sentinel over heart and mind". "He comforteth us in all our mental trouble."

An even deeper problem was moral and spiritual trouble. You must not idealise the apostle. This man had been a blasphemer and a persecutor, "breathing out threatenings and slaughter". If in the moment when he fell from his horse at the Damascus gate he had broken his neck or been trampled to death, it would have been no more (he knew) than he richly deserved. "O wretched man that I am! Who shall deliver me? It is my fault, my own fault, my own most grievous fault, and I am damned to eternal perdition." And it was precisely there that the miracle of the everlasting mercy of Christ had met him, and sent him forth to serve with the passionate gratitude of the forgiven. "He comforteth us in all our moral and spiritual trouble."

Finally, the last great trouble of all – the sting of death, the menace of the king of terrors. It was a haunted civilisation, that ancient world of Greece and Rome, haunted by the grim inexorable shadow of mortality: the last enemy that would be destroyed was death. But "blessed be God!" Paul could cry, "it has been destroyed already! O death, where is thy sting? O grave, where is thy victory?" He will be there to comfort you in the last dark trouble of all.

There is no situation to which it does not apply. This is the illimitable range of the comfort of the Lord.

Put your own experience into it. What is the trouble? Physical? Then the word of the Lord for you is that your physical life – every atom and breath of it – is in the hands of One who knows and cares and understands, who is Himself afflicted in all your afflictions, who is infinitely resourceful and able to make you more than conqueror in every evil day.

Or is it mental? The burden of anxiety? It is always open to you to cast that burden on the Lord, to say to Him every morning, every night – "Father, into Thy hands I commit my spirit," knowing that He will accept responsibility.

Or is it moral and spiritual? Then do believe the central affirmation of your faith, that there is no limit to His love:

> He breaks the power of cancelled sin,
> He sets the prisoner free.

Or is it the shadow of mortality? The Christ of the resurrection is at hand to tell you that what looks like the irrevocable closing of a door and the putting out of a light is in fact the opening of the most wonderful gateway and the sunburst of the most inexpressible glory. In fact, there is no conceivable malady to which this divine therapy does not apply. "Blessed be God, who comforteth us in all our tribulation."

And so we come to the last vital element in Christian comfort which Paul stresses. We have seen the divine source from which it springs, the distinctive character it displays, and the illimitable range it covers. Note finally *the inescapable obligation it imposes*: "that we may be able to comfort them which are in any trouble, by the comfort wherewith we ourselves are comforted of God."

That is vitally important. It means that wherever you see religion self-centred and introverted, clutching the comforts of God to its own particular need and unable to see beyond that – whenever I treat the gospel as a kind of prescription to help me to relax, to secure me against what is difficult and disagreeable – well, it may call itself Christian, but it is an appalling caricature of Christ's intention. The whole purpose, says Paul here, of being comforted by God is that you should now go out and mediate the same gift to other struggling lives that need that comfort badly.

Indeed, the whole mystery of suffering is illuminated here. Do you not think that part at least of the reason for the rough places of life and its sore discipline is to initiate us into the secret of God, that we may through that difficult experience become agents of God's help and encouragement to others? Do you not think it must be God's intention that suffering should be transmuted into love? There is a profound truth surely in the remark that Thornton Wilder puts into the mouth of a character in a play: "In Love's service only the wounded soldiers can serve."

Do you not think that Paul's tormenting handicap, the "thorn in the flesh", and his experience precisely there of God's daily sufficient grace, gave him a power he might otherwise never have possessed to reach and touch other lives? Do you not think the real healers of this ailing world are those whose own peace has been bought with a price? Do you not think this may be part of the redeeming efficacy of the cross of Calvary itself, and that it is because He hung and suffered there that Christ is now and for ever the Saviour of this suffering world?

"He comforts us in all our tribulation, that we may be able to comfort those who are in any trouble by the comfort with which we ourselves are comforted of God." This is the inescapable obligation it imposes. It is an awful thing to worry about self – our security, our success, our social connections – in this tormented world of refugees and racially disinherited folk, with two-thirds of the world's population either undernourished or starving, a world whose tides of loneliness and affliction sweep up to our very own door. It is an awful thing for any Church, any denomination, to be centred upon itself – its status, its prestige, its hoarded venerable traditions – when the whole burden of Christ's message is that the Kingdom of God is so much greater than any Church, any denomination, and that the Church which persists in seeking its own life will certainly lose it in the end. It is so pathetically easy for self to work its way even into the heart of our religious life. But Jesus said, "If any man will come after Me, let him deny himself" – say No to self, and Yes to the will of God in love for the brethren.

> O strengthen me, that, while I stand
> Firm on the rock, and strong in Thee,
> I may stretch out a loving hand
> To wrestlers with the troubled sea.

You will never be nearer Christ than when you are doing that. For after all, where is the Lord Jesus most surely to be found today? Where is what a sacramental theology would call "the real presence of Christ"? No doubt in Word and Sacrament and worship, in all the ordinances of the faith, here in this church, yonder in your own room when you kneel to pray. Yes, but also and most certainly in the flesh and blood of every needy soul throughout God's earth today. This, if only we had eyes to see and a heart to understand, is where Christ the King comes forth to meet us. Did He not tell us this Himself? "I was hungry, and you gave me no meat; sick and in prison, and you visited Me not. Then shall they answer Him, Lord, when saw we Thee hungry or sick or in prison, and did not minister to Thee? Then shall He answer them, Inasmuch as you did it not to one of the least of these, you did it not to Me."

Here is the real presence: every homeless refugee, every hungry child, every racially segregated soul from whom a Western culture stands traditionally and patronisingly aloof; and to come nearer home — that troublesome neighbour, that handicapped sufferer, that poor bungler who has made a wretched mess of his life, that woman who carries a hidden tragedy in her heart, that paganised youth who will tell you he has no use for your religion or your God. This is the real presence; and if we are not prepared to see and serve Him there, in His needy brethren, all our expressions of love to God are worthless and our religious professions frivolous.

Can we face the challenge? The burden of this world's need could break us, the yoke of its callousness crush us — if it were not for one thing: that this is precisely the yoke, the burden, that Christ carried triumphantly through the cross to the resurrection, and is still carrying for ever. So that, in the deepest sense, it is not we who have to be strengtheners and reinforcers of others. It is Christ in us — the living contemporaneous Christ moving out into these other lives. This is the incredible glory of our calling as Christians. And it is along this road that we make the great discovery, that His yoke is easy, and His burden light.

14

HE IS ABLE

"Able to succour them that are tempted."—Hebrews ii. 18.
"Able to save them to the uttermost."—Hebrews vii. 25.
"Able to keep you from falling."—Jude 24.
"Able to subdue all things unto himself."—Philippians iii. 21.
"Able to keep that which I have committed unto him against
that day."—2 Timothy i. 12.
"Able to do exceeding abundantly above all that we ask or think."
—Ephesians iii. 20.

JOHN KEATS in one of his letters uses a vivid, memorable
expression about the literature of Shakespearean England. He
speaks of "the indescribable gusto of the Elizabethan voice".
In an even deeper sense that could be applied to the men of
the New Testament. For if there is one thing more than another
that strikes you about these men it is the fact that they are
possessed by an amazing consciousness of power. They are
intensely, magnificently alive. You cannot fail to feel "the
indescribable gusto" of the early Christian voice.

I doubt whether modern Christianity in some of its manifesta-
tions makes any such impression on the world. It suffers from
too many inhibitions and hesitancies and restraints.

But on every page of the New Testament there meets you a wonderful sense of energy, exhilaration, overpowering vitality. These men are almost uncannily efficient, serenely and superbly adequate to life's most difficult demands.

It is very important to notice their own explanation of this. They never attribute it to anything in themselves. You do not find them strutting about in ostentatious complacency, blustering "We are able!" Once, indeed, James and John did commit themselves to that hazardous assertion, but it was significantly the one occasion when the sons of Zebedee were acting completely out of character, stealing a march on the other disciples and claiming the best places in the Kingdom: hence this is really the exception that proves the rule. No, the constant watchword of the New Testament is not "We are able": what you do find over and over again is "He is able" – and when they say it, they are looking away from themselves to God. They are looking straight at Christ. And on this basis, they proceed to make the most staggering claims. A thousand difficulties may lie across the path: He is able to bring us through! Hot passionate temptations may threaten wreck and ruin: He is able to give the victory! The whole world may seem to be going to the devil, the human race careering headlong to destruction: He is able to bring it to God! All the way through there keeps breaking out the rallying trumpet-note. He is able!

Is this not one main object of our gathering round the Table of the Lord? For the Sacrament summons us to look away from ourselves, away from the strained intent preoccupation with our own dubious resources for life, away from the dreary frustration of wrecked vows and broken dreams – away to a cross towering over the wrecks of time and to a love that has borne our sins in its own body on the tree, and to the living Lord who still comes back to His friends on the first day of the week and communes with them and is known in the breaking of bread. It is on Jesus, crucified and risen, that all our thoughts this day are focused. Beyond our futile striving shines His sufficiency; and beyond our perplexities, His peace. He is able.

I propose, therefore, that we should turn over the pages of the New Testament, and gather out some of the places where this trumpet-note recurs. Let us consider some of the varied situations in life with which we are told "He is able" to deal.

And first, this: "He is able *to succour them that are tempted.*" Certainly those men of the New Testament had first-hand evidence in plenty for this. "Where should I have been," I can imagine Peter saying, "with that hot irascible temper of mine, liable to blaze out disconcertingly and leave behind it a trail of confusion and regret and wounded feelings and resentment — where should I have been, if He had not succoured me there?" And Thomas: "Where should I have been, with my doubts and anxieties and dim forebodings, my frequent midnight wrestling with pessimistic, sceptical moods and bouts of dreary disenchantment — if He had not succoured me there?" And Nicodemus: "Where should I have been, with my groping apprehensive spirit clinging to the shadows, and disinclined in my religion to come out into daylight and broad noon — if He had not succoured me there?" And thousands of others, in Antioch, Ephesus, Corinth, Rome: "Where should we have been, with our masterful sins of the flesh, and our subtle, pervasive sins of the spirit — if Christ had not succoured us there?" "We know this thing is true," they assure us, "it is vouched for in our experience: He is able to succour them that are tempted." And because we are all poor, tempted creatures, this is right on the mark for us.

This writer to the Hebrews let us further into the secret. He tells us how Christ does it. It is because "He Himself hath suffered being tempted". You need never be afraid that Christ will not understand nor enter intimately into your problem and your struggle. Some good people may not — Christ always will.

For His is not the hard, aloof, self-conscious goodness which
repels, because it does not know and has never personally felt
the devastating pressure of the force by which the tempted spirit
is assaulted. He knows about it all. He realises the mettle of the
foe. He understands just how attractive are the insidious and
alluring voices. He has been there, is in fact there with every
struggling soul today. In this Sacrament, He meets us where
we are.

> Didst Thou not in our flesh appear,
>   And live and die below,
> That I may now perceive Thee near,
>   And my Redeemer know?

With a great price He has purchased the right to stand shoulder to shoulder with His brethren in the battle. And one touch
of His all-conquering Spirit can make you more than conqueror. "He is able to succour them that are tempted."

But someone is sure to raise the objection that this is not
sufficient. Doubtless it is a great thing to resist temptation: but
if resistance has already broken down, what then? What about
defeat? Is there any message for that?

Let us turn over the pages and listen for the trumpet note.
We have gone only a page or two when it comes pealing out
again: "He is able *to save to the uttermost.*" This speaks to our
deeper need.

And again they assure us, those men of the New Testament,
that this is not insubstantial talk but proved and verifiable fact.
"I was a blasphemer and a persecutor," declares Paul, "a
blazing red-hot enemy of Christ — and He saved me from that."
"I was a leper," cries another, "segregated from all living
fellowship, cut off from hope and gladness, with my existence a
bleak and solitary misery as this tormented body of mine rotted
slowly to death — and He saved me from that." "I was a helpless

slave in the toils of sin," confesses another, "with my will-power broken, my resolution in ruins, my course set for the ultimate darkness – and He saved me from that." "He is able to save to the uttermost!"

Is there any wonder that the New Testament is punctuated all the way through with sudden lyrical outbursts of doxology, and that ever and again there falls on your ears the shout of a great unnumbered multitude praising and magnifying the Lord?

And this is true not of the New Testament only; for it has found corroboration in every generation since. "I was a wild beast on the coast of Africa," said John Newton, "and Christ saved me." "Look at me," whispered Henry Martyn to those around him as he went down into the river, "the vilest of sinners, yet saved by grace!" "When I die," begged a converted African chief of Dr. Donald Fraser, "write on my tomb the words, Thou has delivered my soul from the lowest hell." Again and again that note rings out: "We know He can do this thing unto the uttermost, for He saved me." "If Thou but speak the word," cried John Wesley to his Lord, "Judas can cast out demons!"

So all the voices are unanimous in their witness that wherever Jesus comes, there is no such thing as irremediable defeat, no tangle that He cannot straighten out, no wounds that will not yield to the great Physician's healing, no lonely outcast who cannot have his feet set this very day upon God's homeward road.

These are the gifts He is offering now as He invites us to His Table. And because there are days in the experience of us all when things have gone wrong and we have known defeat and are feeling utterly depressed; days when, seeing in Christ what we might have been, we are sick at heart because of what we are; when we are so conscious of failure, of the sorry tragic mess in which we have landed ourselves, of our grieving of the·holy and loving Spirit of God, that we doubt whether we can ever be forgiven, or whether there can ever now be any restoration of the years that the locust hath eaten — because of that, we too need this great heartening trumpet-note to come breaking across the confusion of our souls: "He is able to save to the uttermost!" It is the word of the Lord, and it is here in the Sacrament for you. Blessed be His glorious name.

But someone may feel that even this is not sufficient. It is a wonderful thing, no doubt, to have a religion that can raise the fallen and give the defeated a new chance; but is this the best? Must we, then, go on falling and being forgiven? Is that the whole truth about our Christian destiny?

Once again we turn over the pages. Let us listen for the trumpet-note. We have not gone far before we encounter this: "He is able *to keep you from falling*." First, able to succour; then, able to save; and now, able to support.

This means that our holy religion is not simply an ambulance which follows in the wake of battle to deal with casualties. It has another task much more positive and creative and aggressive: it is itself the armour which wins victories. Or, to vary the metaphor, it is not merely the cure for a disease; it is the preventive agent, to preclude the disease from taking hold.

So do not let us tamely accept the miserably depressing doctrine that real moral and spiritual victories are not to be looked for in this present world, and that "failure is the fate appointed". That is less than half the truth. "The curse of religion," wrote that fine spirit Dora Greenwell, "is the habit of translating into a vague future tense what Christ offers us now." The fact is, there are victories within our reach which have the stuff of eternity in them. He is able — now — to keep you from falling.

How God does this is no secret. The Word is made flesh. The divine imperative becomes a Person. Christ takes a man and permeates him with His Spirit. He alters his focus of attention. He supplies new interests. When Christ and His love come

163

in, inevitably other forces go out. Incompatible interests lose their taste and have no more appeal. "This is My body," He is saying to us today, "this is My blood. I give you all I am and have, My life, My love, My very self." It is thus Christ works His will with men, giving new, commanding ideals to live for, and a new master-passion to stand guard over mind and heart. It is thus "He is able to keep you from falling."

But even this, it may be argued, is incomplete. It is a great thing certainly to have a personal religion able to succour, to save, to support: but is that all? Does Christianity end in individualism? Is this succouring and saving and supporting of the individual soul the full range and sweep of Christ's salvation? Has the gospel no wider horizon? Is there no word of the Lord about the chaos of history and the enigma of the world?

There is. I turn over the pages. I listen for the trumpet-note once more. This time it is the apostle Paul who has the trumpet to his lips, and this is the note he sounds: "He is able *to subdue all things to Himself.*"

Never for a moment did those men doubt that Christ's Kingdom was set for victory. They saw Him not only as King of the Church but as King of the world and the universe. Every principality and power would yet go down before Him, every tongue confess Him as Lord of all, every bell in the universe ring out His praise alone.

It seemed the forlornest of forlorn hopes. Christ's Kingdom on earth, to all appearances, was an infinitesimal, pathetic minority movement; and over against it loomed the gigantic shadow of an atheistic totalitarian state. Were these men just romancing, whistling to keep their courage up as they saw the dark descending, indulging in far-fetched fantasy, flamboyant empty rhetoric? "He is able to subdue all things to Himself." How dared they say it, with Rome threatening to sweep them from the earth?

Because of this: they had seen once for all at the cross and the resurrection what God omnipotent could do. There in these two mighty acts, which were really not two but one, they had seen, as in a flash of lightning across the midnight, the glorious truth that nothing could ever stop Jesus now; that the love which had held Him to the cross and the power which had taken Him out of the grave were literally irresistible. Can we not see this too? There where all the concentrated malevolence of darkness, sin, corruption and death has been challenged at the very seat and centre of its power and routed utterly – "made a show of openly", as Paul puts it – there is the irrefragable evidence of Christ's own ultimate claim, "All power is given unto Me in heaven and in earth." "At Augsburg are the powers of hell," said the German princes to Martin Luther, seeking to dissuade him from his perilous venture. But the reformer would have none of that craven capitulation. "And at Augsburg," he shouted, "Jesus reigns!" It is true; and this very Table where we meet today proclaims it. For this is so much more than a memorial feast. Above our gathering shine the words "Until He come." Here is prefigured the great Messianic banquet at the end, when according to His own promise the victory shall be complete and He shall sit down with His people in the Kingdom of God.

> Feast after feast thus comes and passes by,
>   Yet, passing, points to the glad feast above,
> Giving sweet foretaste of the festal joy,
>   The Lamb's great bridal feast of bliss and love.

This is the truth. And you who have seen and understood the cross and the resurrection know the future is secure and the Kingdom founded upon rock. "He is able to subdue all things unto Himself."

But once again someone raises a question-mark. Is this sufficient? Someone will argue thus: "No doubt it is a great thing to be assured that right and truth and the Kingdom of Christ shall conquer at the last, but that is a consummation far away beyond my horizon. I shall be dead long before that happens. And what is the use of talking to me of an everlasting Kingdom or of a racial immortality, if in the meantime death is going to mock my dreams and frustrate the hopes I fight for, if the dear friends I have loved and cared for in this world are carried off into oblivion and so much truth and beauty cast as rubbish to the void, if in fact death is to destroy its countless millions before the one last favoured generation enters the felicity of Utopia?"

This is the question. And it is a momentous question. It lays bare the real sting of our mortality. Life at its best is so fugitive and transient. "In the morning it flourisheth and groweth up; in the evening it is cut down and withereth." Always there is that haunting shadow in the background, always that eerie, ominous silence on the other side of the grave, always that savage triumph of death over life in our mortal flesh. "Never send to know for whom the bell tolls," cried John Donne, preaching in St. Paul's three hundred and fifty years ago, "it tolls for thee!" Is there, then, nothing more? Does the word of the Lord fail us here?

No, indeed. I turn over the pages, listening for the trumpet-note again; and suddenly I hear it. I hear it from a man whose life was almost over, who was lying in prison, facing out towards the violent death he saw inexorably drawing nearer. "He is able *to keep that which I have committed unto Him against that day.*" Add that brave apostolic word to the other notes we have heard already — able to succour, to save, to support, to subdue — and you have this glorious affirmation: Able to secure for ever. "What I have committed to Him" — it is the expression that was used for depositing something precious in a bank for safety —

"He is able to keep against that day." And so death comes to have a different look for all who know the Lord.

> Death's flood hath lost its chill
> Since Jesus crossed the river.
> Lover of souls, from ill
> My passing soul deliver.

There was a day, some three hundred years ago in Edinburgh, when the June sunshine poured into the condemned cell of a prison where James Guthrie, knight of Christ's covenant, was lying. His servant, James Cowie, was with him; and remembering as he awoke that this was to be the day of his dear master's execution, their last day on earth together, he began to weep, as even brave men have wept at the hour of final parting. His weeping aroused his master. "Come, come," said Guthrie gently, "no more of this!" Then pointing to the dancing sunbeams he went on, "This is the day which the Lord hath made; we will rejoice and be glad in it." This is the strong ineffable serenity of the man who has committed his soul to Christ, the Resurrection and the Life. For He, the Vanquisher of death, is able to keep it secure in that last decisive hour.

It is this Master — the Christ of Easter — with whom we hold communion here today. It is not a Dead March the Eucharist needs. It is a Hallelujah Chorus. With trumpet voice the Sacrament proclaims — "Death is swallowed up in victory." "Because I live, ye shall live also."

> The stars shine over the earth,
> The stars shine over the sea,
> The stars look up to the mighty God,
> The stars look down on me;
> The stars will live for a million years,
> For a million years and a day,
> But Christ and I shall live and love
> When the stars have passed away.

167

One thing remains, and this perhaps the loveliest of all. For to the soul that trusts in Him God gives His promise, not only to secure it against the hour of death and judgment, but to surprise and surpass its dreams with the glory of the land beyond the river.

I turn the pages for the last time and hear the trumpet-note once more: "Now unto Him that is able *to do exceedingly abundantly above all that we ask or think*" — far transcending our dreams and throwing into the shade our most audacious hopes — "to Him be glory for ever!"

What can our poor human guesses comprehend of the reality of the life everlasting? Some things indeed we know. We know there will be rest yonder for tired folk, and ampler powers for splendid service in Christ's Kingdom. We know there will be an answer to all the problems and enigmas which have remained unanswered here. We know that separation will be at an end, and that those who have loved on earth will be reunited, to part no more for ever. We know that this corruptible will put on incorruption, and this mortal put on immortality, and — crowning marvel of all — that we shall be presented faultless before the presence of God's glory with exceeding joy.

But beyond this, our time and space conditioned minds just cannot conceive it, and thought falters and imagination fails. We dream. We hope. We look forward. But never forget, says the voice from heaven, that earth's best dreams are but one thousandth part of the glorious reality. To be limited no longer by bodily frustration and by the incubus of long centuries of human ignorance and folly and corruption, to have cast off once for all the shackles of human finitude and sin, to be made in very truth like Christ — what measuring-line ever invented can hope to assess a destiny so transcendent? What can this transitory encampment of our earthly pilgrimage, this poor tent here today and gone tomorrow, tell us of the city which hath foundations, whose builder and maker is God? What can this Table in the wilderness reveal to us of the festal fellowship of heaven? "I go to measure Jerusalem," said the young man of Zechariah's dream. But the prophet heard the Lord God instruct His angel—"Run, speak to this young man, saying, Jerusalem shall be inhabited as towns without walls." Throw your measuring-line away. No use here for that absurd little yardstick of earthly experience. For they who have passed through the gate into the New Jerusalem are at home with Christ for ever; and "He is able to do exceedingly abundantly above all that we ask or think."

There, then, is the watchword of those men of the New Testament and the secret of their amazing, indomitable vitality— never "We are able," but always "He is able." God is able! Christ is able! Able to succour the tempted, able to save to the uttermost, able to support and keep you from falling, able to subdue all things to Himself, able to secure you in death's decisive hour, able to surpass your dreams of immortality. All this is yours and mine, if we are Christ's; and it is all sealed to us in our Sacrament today. Why should we not believe it and confide in it, and lift up our hearts to its splendour? "O house of Jacob, come ye, and let us walk in the light of the Lord!"

> Here faith is ours, and heavenly hope,
>   And grace to lead us higher;
> But there are perfectness and peace
>   Beyond our best desire.
> O by Thy love and anguish, Lord,
>   And by Thy life laid down,
> Grant that we fall not from Thy grace,
>   Nor cast away our crown!

15

THE CHALLENGE
OF HIS COMING

"Teach us what we shall do unto the child that shall be born." —
Judges xiii. 8.

THIS IS THE season of Advent. Advent, properly understood, has three dimensions, past, present and future. The past — Christ's historic coming to Israel at Bethlehem; the present — Christ's constant coming to the Church, and to you and me, in the here and now: the future — Christ's final coming to all the world at the end of the age.

It is the first and second of these we are to think of mainly today. I ask you to consider how Christ's first coming long ago is a type and a parable of His coming to you and me in the here and now.

On these successive Sundays, we sing the Advent hymns and read the Advent scriptures; and thus we climb the slope that leads on and up to Bethlehem. The time draws near the birth of Christ. "What shall we do unto the Child that shall be born?"

There was a day — so this old chronicler of the Book of Judges records — when an angel of the Lord visited Manoah and his wife. He told them they were to expect a child. He told them that the child would be a great leader and deliverer of his people. He would ransom Israel from its captivity. He would break the hereditary enemies, the Philistines. He would be the agent of the divine redeeming strategy.

It was a daunting responsibility to be the parents of such a child. Would God, prayed Manoah, give them a special measure of grace and guidance? Would He show them the way to take, and prepare them to receive aright this babe whose destiny was to be so dramatic? "What shall we do unto the child that shall be born?"

So the child Samson came into the world. So he grew up, and lived and loved and warred and died, and was gathered to his fathers.

Centuries later, the angel of the Lord returned. God was now to send another Deliverer to His people. He, too, would come as a Child. He, too, would ransom captive Israel. He, too, would fight and smash the Philistines: only, His Philistines would not be the warring tribe that once bore that name, but the world, the flesh and the devil, the powers of darkness that corrupt and shackle human life with chains and slavery, the ruthless forces that rot man's soul and bring his brightest visions to the dust.

It was a marvellous divine strategy that laid this Child, Immanuel, upon the doorstep of the world's heart; and immense the responsibility of those who had to receive this gift into their midst. The character of every man and nation, every society and culture, would stand revealed by their attitude to this new act of God. It was indeed — though they might not realise it — the critical, decisive question: "What shall we do to the Child that shall be born?"

Nineteen and a half centuries have passed since then: and still at Advent He draws near, and still at Christmas time He

comes again, the Holy Child of Bethlehem, God impinging on
the human race in Christ – and still the challenge is renewed.
It is a momentous responsibility for our world, our Church, ourselves to face the challenge of His coming.

Historically, there have been three answers to the question.
We are going to look at the Gospel story, and we shall find three
different sets of people giving three conflicting answers. And
these answers have persisted across the centuries, and still repre-
sent the three conflicting attitudes of our contemporary world to
the fact of Christ.

"What shall we do unto the Child that shall be born?" First,
Herod answered it. And his answer? *The answer of hostility.* The
answer of downright antagonism. "Let Him be destroyed! Let
Him die while He is still in His cradle. They say He is a Child
born to be King. King? We shall have no King but Caesar –
and Caesar's deputy, Herod. We shan't brook any interference
with the secular power. If this Child is allowed to grow to
manhood and maturity, who knows how far His menace may
extend? His scale of values and mine will clash at every point.
There is not room for both of us in the same world. Therefore
let Him die while His empire is still a dream. Let Him be destroyed!"

This is Herod's answer: the answer of hostility, the answer
that grew and swelled and multiplied for thirty years till one
day it became a mad mob's terrifying roar – "Away with Him!
Away with Him! Crucify Him!"

It is being given still. For still in the twentieth century as in
the first, the world knows instinctively that a secular society, a
pagan culture, an unredeemed heart are not safe with Christ.
He challenges all their basic axioms.

This is the world's objection to its Messiah. "Gentle Jesus,
meek and mild" – that would be all right: no danger there.
An unworldly, mystical dreamer – better still. A stained-glass

172

window Christ, who will never come down from His stained-glass to trouble you—best of all. But a regnant Christ, an invading Christ, a life-revolutionising Christ—that is intolerable. That menaces our way of life, damages our self-determination, strikes at the roots of our independence. If this formidable invasion is not repudiated from the start, there is no saying how it may inhibit our liberty of action. Away with Him! We will not have this Man to reign over us. Let Him and His Kingdom be destroyed!

This is the situation. And it is well that we should recognise it. This is the precise assault our holy faith is meeting in many lands, even when the Christmas carols are calling men to Bethlehem. This is the context of crisis in which the Church goes out on mission to the world. This is the fierce, determined, nihilistic opposition.

Is this a pessimistic outlook? On the contrary. It is a future we can face with lifted heads. Zion has looked into the cold, hostile eyes of Babylon before now. And the faith which once, while still in its cradle, met the withering blast of a militant totalitarian atheism has no need now, when God has blessed it in the earth, to feel unready or dismayed.

That on the wider scale. What of the more personal issue? For there is a personal issue here. "What shall we do to the Child that shall be born?" We have heard the answer of Herod, the answer of hostility. Thank heaven, we say, we have never given that answer. No. And yet—I wonder. Is it perhaps possible sometimes to fight against Christ without knowing that we are doing it? If ever when God's clear guidance has come to us—"This is the way, walk ye in it"—we have turned aside and chosen another path of our own devising; if ever, having some conscience about goodness and honour, we have done violence to that conscience and smothered the still small voice and sinned against the light—then we, too, have stood with the enemy and given our judgment against Christ. And "if"—as the

Master put it — "the light that is in thee be darkness, how great is that darkness!"

"What shall we do to the Child that shall be born?" I say now there was another question Herod ought to have been asking. He ought to have asked, "What shall the Child that is to be born do to me?" This is the divine paradox of the Gospel story. This is the blazing irony of the incarnation. Across those lovely hopes of Bethlehem, the shadow of the tyrant loomed vast and ominous and terrific, and the Babe seemed weak and helpless. But history bears witness that when the proud tyrant in his might struck out at Mary's Child he was striking — unknown to himself — at the elemental force of the universe. He was pitting himself against the drive of the purpose of Almighty God. And it broke him utterly.

This is the eternal fact. To repudiate the moral values of Jesus Christ is not to join issue with a dim dead figure of a distant past: it is to take arms against "the everlasting right" for which "the silent stars are strong". And that is always a hopeless warfare.

Don't we ourselves know from bitter experience that every time we tamper with integrity and break troth with Jesus we are complicating our life and darkening our skies, confusing the eternal issues and throwing our true happiness away?

Therefore: "Search me, O God, and know my heart; try me, and know my thoughts" — try me in the light of Bethlehem, search me with the judgment and the mercy of Immanuel — "and see if there be any wicked way in me, and lead me in the way everlasting."

Let us pass on. Herod's was not the only answer, then or now. Let us listen to another.

"What shall we do to the Child that shall be born?" *The Bethlehem innkeeper* answered it. And his answer? Not hostility. Not opposition. No. *The answer of secular preoccupation.* "Do?

174

What shall I do? With the best will in the world, there is little or nothing I can do. My house is crowded, my hands full, my mind preoccupied. I wish I could help them, but I must keep a due sense of priorities. After all, this coming Child is no real concern of mine. I am sorry. I am not a hardhearted man. There is the stable – they are welcome to it, if they care to use it; but that is the best we can do. And now I must get back to my work. My guests are needing me. This other matter I must dismiss from my thoughts."

This is the innkeeper's answer, the answer of preoccupation, the answer the Child was destined to meet again and again all through His days on earth. Not fierce opposition, not furious hatred, but inattention and unconcern – secular priorities inducing apathy. And when His days on earth were over, what was this Messiah to the majority of His race? Neither an object of fervent devotion, nor a target of passionate animosity – but less than the dust beneath time's chariot wheels. He just did not matter at all. He could be ignored.

It is being given still, this answer. For still in the twentieth century as in the first there are multitudes for whom the faith is neither a miracle nor a menace, but simply an irrelevance: people who say – "You surely don't expect us to believe that a birth nineteen hundred years ago has any bearing on our besieging problems and bewilderments today? We are living in a totally different universe now, infinitely vaster, dizzyingly, staggeringly greater in time and space than the ancients who wrote the Bible ever knew, dwarfing all your traditional beliefs and pieties into the insignificance and irrelevance of an archaeological pedantry. Oh, of course," they may add, "we have no objection to your indulging in worship and prayer; go on with your visitation evangelism and your foreign missions or what you will; keep your Church wheels turning, for all we care. But don't ask us to commit intellectual suicide by taking it seriously. What have churches, creeds, sacraments to do with us? The forgiveness of sins, the practice of the presence of God, the communion of saints – all that is outside our orbit completely, not our line of territory at all. We realists have more urgent business on our hands than credulously waiting upon a God who perhaps does not exist. The hope of the world, this Jesus? Let Him be ignored!"

The answer of preoccupied indifference. Now, of course, it would be easy to denounce it, easy to show the irrationality of this garbled rationalism. But before we do that, there is a question we had better ask. Is it possible that we Christians are partly to blame for its prevalence? Is this what has happened – that too much conventional church religion devoid of zeal and glow and power, too much apologising Christianity lacking the authentic notes of certainty, finality and joy, have given the world the impression that Christ makes very little difference after all? Is it that the divisions within the Church, our concentration on secondary things, our failure to speak out and give a strong prophetic lead above the tumult and the shouting of conflicting policies in this nuclear age, our needless petty rivalries, have seemed to suggest that the faith itself is petty? Is it that our distinctive claims are belied by our undistinctive practice, and made to look ridiculously exaggerated? "These Christians," growled Nietzsche once, "must show me that they are redeemed before I will believe in their Redeemer!" Should not our Advent prayer be this – "O God, end our dull, tedious misrepresenting of the faith, and set us on fire for Christ!"

But the main reason is different. When men ignore Christ today, it is because – like the Bethlehem innkeeper – they cannot find room for Him. All the accommodation is already taken up by other crowding interests. It is not atheism, though that may be given as the ostensible reason. It is not defiant anti-religion. It is preoccupation, and the feeling of being able to get on reasonably well without the things of which religion speaks. "What shall we do with the Child?" Some may cry "Crown

176

Him!"—others "Crucify Him!" But far more there are who prefer the middle way: Let Him be ignored.

But now here is the fallacy in that position. Here is the illogicality of indifference. Christ refuses to be ignored.

Look at it like this. There are indeed myriads of facts in this world you can disregard, multitudes of events you do not need to come to terms with. They lay no compelling hands upon you. The politics of Julius Caesar, the origins of the sonnet, the tactics of Waterloo, the internal motions of the planetary nebulae—such things do not enter directly into the structure of my everyday experience. I can ignore them. I can disregard them. But there are other facts that will not thus be disregarded. I cannot indefinitely ignore the laws of health, the social solidarity of the community, the demands of duty, the reality of death. I cannot ignore the basic truth that "whatsoever a man soweth that shall he also reap". And of all the facts in life that refuse to be ignored, the greatest by far is Jesus Christ.

He haunts the human race. Men have tried for nineteen centuries to escape Him, and after all their trying He pursues them still. I know that if I take the wings of the morning and dwell in the uttermost parts of the sea, I shall find Him there. I know that whether civilisation climbs the steep ascent of heaven or plunges down to hell, it will find Him there. The world may flout His laws, and trample His name in the dust of oblivion: I can wash my hands of Him, like Pilate, and drug my soul in slumber and apostasy. But irresistibly and inexorably He comes back, our Judge and our Redeemer, our Tormentor and our Saviour, the pressure of Almighty God on your life and mine, He comes back and stands at the door and knocks. He is there now—this Advent season—and He will not be ignored. "Lo, I am with you always, even unto the end of the world."

Let us pass on once again. Herod's answer and the

innkeeper's answer were not the only answers, then or now. Let us listen to one more.

"What shall we do unto the Child that shall be born?" *Simeon in the temple* answered it. The old saint of God who took the Child into his arms answered it. *The answer of commitment.* The answer of complete devotion. For when Joseph and Mary brought the Child on the day of dedication, this man by some inner vision knew and hailed Him and thanked God for His unspeakable gift. "Mine eyes have seen Thy salvation."

This is Simeon's answer: the answer of commitment.

It is being given still. I pray God it may be given today.

This is no time – when atheism is militant and the spirit of denial is passionate and missionary – for any follower of Jesus to be vague and dispassionate in allegiance. Simeon embraced God's Messiah. He took Him to his heart. Do we?

Doubtless in a sense we do. We give Him a place of honour in our life. We should not be here today if we were not doing that. We certainly should not wish to face life with Jesus Christ left out. But – the absolutely central place? I wonder. Admiration? Yes, indeed. Support and backing? Yes, by all means. But decisive surrender? Downright commitment? The resolute determination that in all things, whatever the cost, He shall have the pre-eminence? It is possible to be in Jesus' camp – camp-followers – yet not passionately on His side.

The fact of the matter is – if the Church needs Advent and Christmas, quite desperately it needs Pentecost too. It needs to have its natural competence and fidelity supernaturalised. It needs to get its logic set on fire. It needs to see its doctrinal patterns and theological precision shaken by the winds of heaven. It needs more than the routine devotion of a random venture. It needs the intent purposefulness of a master-passion.

And I do not see how that is ever going to come upon the Church, or on you and me who are the Church – unless and until we allow the magnificence of our holy faith to smite us with its glory and burn us with its flame.

We believe our creed. But belief is not enough. Have we *imagined* it? Have we realised it? Are we seeing its truth? Are we taking time to be still and know that it is true, and to exult in its splendid relevance?

It is true that at the first Advent:

> He came down to earth from heaven
> Who is God and Lord of all.

It is true that He bore my sins and yours in His own body on the tree. It is true that death could not hold Him, and that He was resurrected by the power of God. It is true that He is alive and out on all the roads of the world today, mighty to save. It is true that He is here in this church at this moment, and that if only we were not fast held behind the gates of sense and flesh we should actually see Him here, face to face, now. It is true that He can take our lives and interpenetrate them with His own, to enable us to say, "I live, yet not I, but Christ liveth in me." It is true that one day we are going to see Him face to face without any veil at all.

These things are true. And you believe them. But today I am begging you not only to believe them — but to imagine them, to visualise them, to see them, and to act on the basis of them. For it is as we let the shining, supercharged truth of them get hold of us, really take possession of us, that like Simeon we shall meet Christ reborn for us this Advent time.

And then? Why then, what does it matter whether life be long or short? If it is to be a long day's strenuous march, what joy, O Christ, to have Thy blessed companionship all the way! If it is to be a brief moment and a sudden call — "Lord, now lettest Thou Thy servant depart in peace, for mine eyes have seen Thy salvation."

16

WHAT THE SPIRIT
IS SAYING TO THE CHURCHES

"He that hath an ear, let him hear what the Spirit saith unto the churches." —Revelation ii. 7.

THE SPIRIT IS assuredly saying some radical things to the churches today. There is a stirring in the life of all the churches which means that God the Holy Ghost is speaking. Through the tumult and the shouting of international controversy, through the clash and the clang of modern materialist civilisation, through the tangled complexity of ecclesiastical debate, through the problems and bewilderments of our own hearts, a deeper note keeps beating — the Spirit of God crying to those who have ears to hear.

John wrote to seven churches in Asia, not because there were only seven (for actually there were far more), not because these seven lay geographically in a circle, but because seven is symbolical — it is the perfect number — so that in writing to these seven he writes to all, to the Church Universal, to all congregations of Christian people scattered everywhere throughout the world: to Britain and America, to Germany and Africa and India. We ourselves are part of this. He writes to you and me.

Now each of the letters has one distinctive note, a single operative word or vital challenging phrase to sum up the whole message. I suggest that we should listen to these different notes: for they will give us what the Holy Spirit is saying to the churches now.

Here, to begin with, is Ephesus. What does the Spirit say to the church in Ephesus? The Spirit says—"*Repent.*" "Thou hast left thy first love: remember, therefore, and repent."

Now think of the Church anywhere—Ephesus, Geneva, Canterbury, Edinburgh, New York. We are the Church of four mighty historical acts: the Church of the Incarnation, of the Cross, of the Resurrection, of Pentecost. Can we measure up to any of these descriptions of the Church without penitence and contrition?

The Church of the Incarnation—of the Word who was made flesh, who never stood aloof in a superior holiness, but gladly came right down for love of men into the fearful pit and the miry clay and the multiple miseries of all mankind, right into a world that had things in it as frightful as Belsen and Buchenwald and Hiroshima; and all the outcasts felt at home with Him, and He called the harlots friends. We are hardly like that, are we, with our too often disincarnate pieties, our disembodied theologies, our ecclesiastical self-segregation, our rationalising busyness designed precisely to avoid the embarrassment of giving ourselves away? Church of the Incarnation, says the Holy Spirit, remember and repent!

The Church of the Cross: and not, mark you, the cross of the stained-glass window and the silver ornament, not the cross about which it is all too easy to wax eloquent or even sentimental. But the cross which for Jesus meant total abnegation, stark and painful, total reversal of the world's whole scale of values, self just blotted out. We are not like that normally, who so easily become infected in the Church by secular ideas of what constitutes prosperity and success and importance and security. Church of the Cross, says the Spirit, remember and repent!

The Church of the Resurrection. That is to say, the Church of the greatest, gladdest, best of news that ever startled men's ears and shattered the midnight of their souls. The Church that once went singing through the world and shouting through the martyr fires — "He is risen. Hallelujah — Christ is risen!" We are not like that, are we, who contrive to take our holy faith so dreadfully sedately, submerged in our dull tedious routine? Church of the Resurrection, remember and repent!

The Church of Pentecost: Pentecost, where men heard the rushing mighty wind and saw the descending fire; where they spoke in new tongues of the wonderful works of God; where they were all with one accord in one place, welded into the most vital unity of fellowship the world has ever seen. We are not like that, are we? — we who feel ashamed sometimes at our supineness and shocked at our divisions: and I mean shocked not merely at their waste and stupidity, but shocked at their sinfulness. For the Lord God is calling us to go out and preach reconciliation to the nations, to society, to all the broken lives of men: and how can we preach it when we are notoriously divided ourselves? Certainly the difficulties are real and formidable, admitting of no facile solution. But the fact remains that there are doctrines we hold in common, and facts which these doctrines enshrine, so incomparably miraculous, so world-shattering in their significance, so humanly speaking incredible, that they dwarf everything that keeps us apart. If we really believe the great facts of our faith — incarnation, atonement, resurrection — not vaguely assenting to them as articles in a creed but truly imagining them and seeing them, held and possessed by them, must they not outweigh everything else, and must not their uniting power be stronger than the centrifugal forces that rend the Church asunder? Can we go on indefinitely debating secondary things, with Christ standing there declaring "Before Abraham was, I am"? It appears that we can. This is the catastrophic stubbornness of human sin. And it just will not do to pride ourselves that we at least do not create the problem, that all the barriers are on the other side of some ecclesiastical fence; for that is to thank God that we are not as other men and churches are—and is there not a parable of Jesus to say that that is precisely the sin that can most effectively damn the soul? Church of Pentecost, remember and repent!

This is the word for the Church in Ephesus: Repent. And he that hath an ear, let him hear what the Spirit is saying to the churches.

Here is Smyrna. What does the Spirit say to the Church in Smyrna? The Spirit says—*"Realise your riches."* "I know your poverty, but you are rich."

Now this might be called the very signature tune of the New Testament. The New Testament is not a dull treatise on ethical theism or mild humanitarianism or respectable behaviour. It is much more like a wild treasure island story, throbbing with the exhilaration of stupendous discovery, fabulous wealth, colossal unsearchable riches. And mark you, this is not fairy-tale and make-believe. That God bears the sins of the world, this—even in a world of electronic brains and artificial satellites and technical marvels of all kinds—is the ultimate mystery and the irrefragable truth. That Christ communicates life—this is the redeeming of existence from meaninglessness and insignificance. For the moment you can say—"I live, yet not I, but Christ liveth in me," you are into a new dimension. Your human nature has been laid hold of by super-nature. To use our Lord's own figure, just as the vine injects its life into the branch, so Christ imparts to His Church and to all who will receive Him the very life of God: not just an improved existence, but actually God's own quality of life.

The trouble is that we will not believe it. Hence you get the appalling difference between the magnificent audacity of the Church's creed and the dull conventionality of its life. It is because we do not fully believe it that we are all at sixes and sevens. And so when Julian Huxley at the University of Chicago's Darwinian centenary celebrations prophesied the emergence of a new religion without revelation or the supernatural, or Earl Russell tells us "Why I am not a Christian," when one school of psychology sponsors "morals without religion" and another expounds conversion in terms of brain-washing, there are Christians who start trembling for the ark of God. It is so absurdly unnecessary. For as "heirs of God, joint-heirs with Christ," we hold the title-deeds of our inheritance here and now, life eternal in the midst of time, the first anticipatory sample and instalment of the heavenly Kingdom: so that all the arguments of all the Huxleys and Russells and death-of-God theologians are impotent and ineffective and ultimately irrelevant.

> Come, Almighty to deliver,
> Let us all Thy life receive.

This is the word for the Church in Smyrna: Realise your riches. And he that hath an ear, let him hear what the Spirit is saying to the churches.

Here is Pergamos. What does the Spirit say to the Church at Pergamos? The Spirit says — "*Stand for freedom!*" He says — "Resist the encroaching pressure of power politics and pagan ideologies." For this is the meaning of the cryptic double reference to "Satan's throne." "You have to live your life," he tells them twice over, "where Satan sits enthroned": an oblique reference to the Caesar worship of the imperial cult at Pergamos, in which a militant totalitarian political secularism loomed with a baleful hatred upon the men and women who were Christ's Church. Stand for freedom!

Ancient history? It is nothing of the kind. I think of our

fellow-Christians in China, with the perpetual problem confronting them — "How far can we go with the present government, and where have we to stop and refuse to collaborate, saying 'Here stand I; I can no other; so help me God'?" I think of our fellow-Christians in certain parts of Africa, some of them dictated to by a totalitarian law which says "You may worship in this church but not in that" — as though the Church could be ordered about by a Department of State and were not the house of the living God, the pillar and ground of the truth. I think of the pressures there are in present-day society to get people, young people especially, to consent to and acquiesce in sub-Christian standards of culture: "Conform, or be left out!" — which is secularism's dreary reversal of the ancient word, "Be not conformed to this world, but be transformed by the renewing of your mind." I think of one of the greatest and most urgent of international problems, the question of the proliferation of nuclear weapons and the dangers of nuclear tests. Christians may take one side or another quite sincerely. There are diversities of judgment here. But at least we are bound to say this, that if any Christian, after deep, long searching of his soul and endeavouring to find the mind of Christ, should feel moved to speak out for abolition of such tests, and then encounters the contemptuous retort that he is a poor dupe, a misguided meddler, an unconscious victim of alien subtle propaganda — this at any rate is a libel and a lie. "Son of man, stand upon thy feet!"

This is the word for the Church at Pergamos: Stand for freedom. And he that hath an ear, let him hear what the Spirit is saying to the churches.

Here is Thyatira. What does the Spirit say to the Church at Thyatira? The Spirit says — *"Hold fast."* "That which ye have already hold fast till I come." This is Christian tenacity, that essential ingredient of discipleship. Hold out to the end!

Have you ever noticed, in reading the *Pilgrim's Progress,* how often Bunyan's pilgrim Christian, in journeying to the Celestial city, was met by pilgrims going the wrong way — like Timorous and Mistrust, who came running down the road shouting to him "Go back, man, go back! There are lions in the path!" — or like Mr. Pliable, who indeed made a splendid and encouraging beginning to the pilgrimage, outstripping the rest in his enthusiasm, until one day the Slough of Despond got hold of him, and he climbed out on the side nearest his own house, a pathetic, mud-bedraggled thing, and made tracks for home, and was never seen again?

That is the great danger — that you and I should lose heart in following Christ our King, and in the lengthening shadows should stand thinking back regretfully to the joy and confidence and dedication of earlier days now gone beyond recall, vanished in the devastating attrition of the years. When Paul wrote about Christians "starting in the Spirit and ending in the flesh" — which means, starting with devotion and ending with drudgery — he was referring to a risk from which none of us is immune.

> Whither is fled the visionary gleam?
> Where is it now, the glory and the dream?

It is pathetic; and the reason why it is so pathetic is precisely that it is utterly unnecessary. For this world has Pentecost in it. It is not a matter of summoning up our own resources. It is a matter of accepting God's gift. Why should we go on trying to live the Christian life in our own strength, when all the time God is offering us through the channels of prayer and dedication a resource and capacity of a totally different kind, new every morning, the identical power that made the men of Pentecost more than conquerors? This is the secret of serving Christ as long as life shall last with fresh, unwearied spirit. "They go from strength to strength; every one of them in Zion appeareth before God."

This is the word for the Church at Thyatira: Hold fast. And he that hath an ear, let him hear what the Spirit is saying to the churches.

Here is Sardis. What does the Spirit say to the Church at Sardis? The Spirit says—"*Beware of nominal Christianity*". "Thou hast a name that thou livest"—you are nominally alive —"and art dead." You have all the paraphernalia of religion, the machinery, the organisation; but the vital spark, the life, the creative, dynamic thing is not there.

That, at Sardis, was the tragedy. For as a rule what amazed and troubled and discomfited the Roman Empire about early Christianity was precisely its vitality. If they tried to put it down here, it would break out there. Wherever they touched it, they got something like an electric shock. "Look out," they began to say, "this new movement is dangerous. The thing's alive!"

But not here. Not at Sardis. "You have a name to live"— you are nominally Christian, but the lustre has gone: the thing is not real!

Something must have happened in Sardis akin to what Albert Schweitzer said has been happening in our modern world. Look, said Schweitzer, at what the modern world has done to the great imperious demands of Jesus in the gospels. "Many of the greatest sayings are found lying in a corner like explosive shells from which the charges have been removed."

Paul told the Corinthians, "I may have this, and that, and the next thing, but if I have not love I am nothing." Similarly, what the Spirit is saying to the churches and telling some of us in the depths of our own hearts is this: I can have all the nominal Christianity in the world, but if I have not the life of Jesus I am nothing. I can intellectualise my religion, debating endlessly in discussion group the intricacies of creation and redemption, predestination and free will; I can legalise it, stressing the obligation of church attendance, Sabbath observance and so forth; I can institutionalise it, multiplying the apparatus of meetings and activities; I can standardise it, ritualise it, socialise it – but it is all worth precisely nothing, if I have not in me the life, the very life, of Jesus. "Nothing," wrote Kierkegaard, "is more dangerous to true Christianity than to get men to assume lightmindedly the name of Christian, as if it were something that one is as a matter of course." Hence we ought to be immensely grateful that in the Spirit poured out upon the Church at Pentecost there is the divine antidote to all dull, competent, lustreless religion, the shattering of complacency and the end of being nominally Christian. "If ye know how to give good gifts to your children, how much more will your heavenly Father give the Holy Spirit to them that ask Him!"

This is the word for the Church at Sardis: Beware of nominal Christianity. And he that hath an ear, let him hear what the Spirit is saying to the churches.

Here is Philadelphia. What does the Spirit say to the Church at Philadelphia? The Spirit says – *"Evangelise!"* "Behold, I have set before thee an open door, and no man can shut it." Go out and evangelise! The very geographical position of Philadelphia gave this church a unique evangelising opportunity. For Philadelphia stood at the head of the valley through which the great route from the western sea climbed to the hinterland of the central Asian plateau – the open door towards the cosmopolitan cities and commerce of the Orient. Philadelphia was the keeper of the gateway. And the Spirit says now to the Church – That is your vocation: to go right out through that open gateway, not to sit down content in some cosy Christian circle of like-minded people, insulated against the swarming life of the great secular world, the bewilderments of space-age man and the massive resurgence of non-Christian faiths; not to be

> a garden walled around,
> A little spot enclosed by grace
> Out of the world's wide wilderness,

but to be an expeditionary force, infiltrating the world of business and commerce and society in the name of Jesus. I have set before you an open door. Evangelise!

But what is modern evangelism? Mass meetings? Yes, certainly there is still a place for this. But surely something more. The House Church? The industrial mission? Vocational and visitation evangelism? All this indeed: but surely something more. Evangelism is a fellowship of reconciled and forgiven sinners feeling a personal responsibility and concern to make real to all men everywhere the reconciliation and forgiveness of God. Was it not William Temple who declared – "The Church exists primarily for those who never go near it"? The real tragedy is when a church is not worried about those who never go near it, is quite content to leave the line of demarcation intact, looks askance at those outwith its own spiritual like-minded family circle, maintains a mute, aloof, condemnatory apartheid from the secularism round its doors. In an introverted way that church may be flourishing, but it is certainly not Christian. What was the symbolism, asks the writer to the Hebrews, of Jesus' dying outside the gate, outside the camp, outside the walls of the holy city of Jerusalem? And he answers his own question. It is that we should now feel an irresistible constraint to "go forth to Him outside the camp, bearing His reproach". It is to burn it into our conscience that this is the surest place where Christ is to be found today, out in the world He died to redeem, and that to stay in the camp is to lose Him. Let me put it as bluntly as I can by saying this. Every time we raise a barrier of aloofness and condemnation between ourselves and the outside world, we are doing exactly what the man did in Jesus' parable who, having been pardoned by his master a frightful debt of a million pounds, could not forget that his neighbour owed him a wretched, paltry five-pound note. And Jesus said that that is the kind of righteousness that books a man for hell. This surely is evangelism, to have learned to say —"Who am I to condemn, when God has forgiven me so hugely?" This is evangelism: a reconciled, forgiven Church not simply preaching, but living and offering to all men, the reconciliation and forgiveness of God.

This is the word for the Church at Philadelphia: Evangelise. And he that hath an ear, let him hear what the Spirit is saying to the churches.

Finally, here is Laodicea. What does the Spirit say to the Church at Laodicea? The Spirit says —"*Warm your faith at the fire of Jesus Christ.*" Laodicea was told she was neither hot nor cold but simply tepid. It is not at all polite language here: I can't help that. "Because you are lukewarm, and neither cold nor hot, because your religion is tepid, you make Me sick!"

It is good that the risen Christ should employ such a devastating form of rebuke. For what chance has a tepid Christianity today? The opposition to Christianity is certainly not tepid. It is scorching.

Hence it is surely terribly foolish to suggest, as is sometimes done, that what is mainly needed for a renewal of the Church is an overhaul of the machinery of Church courts, or a democratisation of Church Committees, or a resuscitation of the parochial system. All that may be necessary enough; but we need so much more — not a blueprint but a resurrection trumpet, not a few Acts of Assembly but the kindling contact of the flame of heaven. "Without enthusiasm," cried Joseph Parker once, "what is the Church? It is Vesuvius without fire, it is Niagara without water, it is the firmament without the sun!"

We know this is the Church's need because we know it is our own. Each one of us would confess — "Lord, I have been such a poor specimen of what Your love can do, such a misleading advertisement of Your power." But we believe in the Holy Ghost. And we are here, all of us together, God's raw material for the building of His Kingdom. And Christ still moves, as John saw Him, among the seven golden candlesticks or lampstands: He is still the One, the only One, who can make the churches shine or any cold heart catch fire.

This is the word for the Church at Laodicea: Warm your faith at the fire of Jesus Christ. Or, turning it into a prayer, as each of us well might do: "O Light of all the world, relight my lamp today."

> Father, forgive the cold love of the years
>   As here in the silence we bow;
> Perish our cowardice, perish our fears,
>   Kindle us, kindle us now.
>
> Lord, we accept, we believe, we adore,
>   Less than the least though we be;
> Fire of love, burn in us, burn evermore
>   Till we burn out for Thee.

And he that hath an ear, let him hear what the Spirit is saying to the churches.

Faith : Reason

* Must you understand the mechanics — the psyco - dynamics of breathing before you draw a breath? Most of us do not yet — If so — you're dead; never say understand.

Or. we breathe — as is natural; required. And while we breathe come to understand? No breath, death. To do — makes understanding possible. Even so must one draw life thru faith — ; when alive — : only then — can one come to understand; know the thing of the Spirit.

(163. use Sun.) 188 bulletin

176 bulletin

scientific humanism
Last week we spent most of our time
on the word belief — or what it all
hangs in John, I'm thru "faith" that we enters
Eternal life; no other way.